the tomato basket

the tomato basket

more than 75 deliciously different ways
to prepare, eat and enjoy the tomato
in all its glorious variety

Jenny Linford

photography by **Peter Cassidy**

RYLAND PETERS & SMALL
LONDON • NEW YORK

To my husband Chris and
my son Ben, with my love

Senior Designer Sonya Nathoo
Picture Manager Christina Borsi
Commissioning Editor Stephanie Milner
Production Controller Sarah Kulasek-Boyd
Art Director Leslie Harrington
Editorial Director Julia Charles
Publisher Cindy Richards

Food Stylist Lizzie Harris
Prop Stylist Joanna Harris
Indexer Vanessa Bird

First published in the United Kingdom
in 2015 by Ryland Peters & Small
20–21 Jockey's Fields
London WC1R 4BW
and
341 East 116th Street
New York NY 10029
www.rylandpeters.com

Text © Jenny Linford 2015
Design and photographs (except
for those credited on page 159)
© Ryland Peters & Small 2015

ISBN: 978-1-84975-598-6

1 0 9 8 7 6 5 4 3 2

Printed and bound in China.

A CIP record for this book is available from
the British Library. CIP data from the Library
of Congress has been applied for.

NOTES
• Both British (Metric) and American
(Imperial plus US cups) are included in
these recipes for your convenience,
however it is important to work with one
set of measurements and not alternate
between the two within a recipe.
• All spoon measurements are level unless
otherwise specified.
• All eggs are medium (UK) or large (US),
unless specified as large, in which case US
extra-large should be used. Uncooked or
partially cooked eggs should not be served
to the very old, frail, young children,
pregnant women or those with
compromised immune systems.
• Ovens should be preheated to the
specified temperatures. We recommend
using an oven thermometer. If using a fan-
assisted oven, adjust temperatures
according to the manufacturer's
instructions.
• Whenever butter is called for within these
recipes, unsalted butter should be used.
• When a recipe calls for the grated
zest of citrus fruit, buy unwaxed fruit and
wash well before using. If you can only find
treated fruit, scrub well in warm soapy
water before using.
• To sterilize preserving jars, wash them
in hot, soapy water and rinse in boiling
water. Place in a large saucepan and cover
with hot water. With the saucepan lid
on, bring the water to a boil and continue
boiling for 15 minutes. Turn off the heat
and leave the jars in the hot water until just
before they are to be filled. Invert the jars
onto a clean dish towel to dry. Sterilize the
lids for 5 minutes, by boiling or according to
the manufacturer's instructions. Jars should
be filled and sealed while they are still hot.

Contents

Introduction

The tale of the tomato is an extraordinary success story. Today, the tomato is a key ingredient in a globe-trotting array of cuisines around the world. Juicy-fleshed and delicate in flavour, offering a distinctive blend of acidity and sweetness, the tomato is a wonderfully versatile food – incidentally available in hundreds of varieties – able to be eaten raw in dishes such as salads and salsas and also cooked in soups, sauces and curries. It can be a major element in dishes, such as gazpacho or tomato sauce for pasta, or a cheerful bit-player, livening up salads, breads, stews and dals.

The story of the tomato plant (*Solanum lycopersicum*), a member of the family *Solanaceae*, begins in South America, from where it originates. From there it travelled north, cultivated by the Aztecs in Mexico around 700 AD. The word 'tomato' derives from the Aztec name *xitomatl*. Botanically speaking, the tomato is the fruit of the plant, but in culinary terms it is perceived as a vegetable. It is thought that the Spanish Conquistadors who invaded Mexico introduced tomato plants from the New World to Europe in the 16th century. Initially, this mysterious new plant was credited with aphrodisiac powers, hence its French nickname *pomme d'amour* or 'apple of love'. In Italian, *pomodoro*, meaning 'golden apple' is a reference to the myth of Hesperides.

The tomato is used in many cuisines, but is particularly associated with Italian cuisine, where it features in many classic dishes. Appropriately, therefore, the first published reference to *mala aurea*, 'golden apples', is in an Italian herbal in 1544. Southern Italy, Naples and the area around it, is particularly associated with the tomato, as this is where the prized San Marzano variety was traditionally cultivated. Naples is, of course, famously known as the home of pizza, and the classic Pizza Napoletana features a signature smear of tasty red tomato sauce as well as mozzarella cheese.

One reason why the tomato is so ubiquitous in kitchens around the world is our ability to preserve. The process of canning tomatoes, so enabling them to be eaten outside their natural season, developed in the 19th century, notably in America as well as in Italy. Now, canned tomatoes, either whole or chopped, and tubes of concentrated tomato purée/paste are store-cupboard staples. Not only is it a useful and popular vegetable, it is one for which many positive health claims are made. Tomatoes are high in vitamins A and C and rich in lycopene, the plant pigment that makes them red, an antioxidant credited with many valuable, health properties.

Writing this book brought home to me just what a wonderful ingredient the tomato is. Often taken for granted, it is a food to be celebrated and enjoyed. Happy cooking!

small bites

Classic gazpacho

A classic Spanish chilled soup, this is a wonderfully refreshing dish to enjoy on a hot summer's day. As it needs to be made in advance, ideally a day ahead, it's excellent for entertaining.

1 kg/2¼ lbs. ripe tomatoes

1 roasted red (bell) pepper, peeled, deseeded and chopped

1 garlic clove, peeled and chopped

1 shallot or ½ onion, peeled and chopped

½ cucumber, chopped

150 ml/⅔ cup tomato juice

100 ml/scant ½ cup extra virgin olive oil

2 tablespoons red wine vinegar

salt and caster/superfine sugar, to taste

Garnish

3 slices rustic bread, crusts trimmed, and diced

½ yellow (bell) pepper, finely diced

¼ cucumber, finely diced

edible micro shoots, to garnish (optional)

Serves 12

Begin by scalding the tomatoes following the instructions on page 17. Chop the flesh and transfer to a food processor. Blend the tomatoes together with the (bell) pepper, garlic, shallot and cucumber until finely chopped, but with some texture. Transfer the mixture to a serving bowl and stir in the tomato juice, 75 ml/⅓ cup of the oil and the vinegar. Season to taste with salt and sugar. Cover and chill in the fridge overnight.

To make the croutons, heat the remaining oil in a small frying pan/skillet over a medium heat and sauté the bread until golden on all sides. Remove from the pan and set aside to cool.

Serve the gazpacho cold in small bowls, topped with the croutons, yellow pepper and cucumber. Garnish with micro shoots and serve at once.

Bloody Mary prawn cocktail

A little advance planning is needed for this tipsy take on the prawn/shrimp cocktail, as the tomatoes need time to marinate. Serve as a distinctly grown-up appetizer.

14 baby plum tomatoes

1½ tablespoons vodka

a dash of Worcestershire sauce

1 teaspoon Tabasco sauce

2 tablespoons mayonnaise

2 teaspoons tomato purée/paste

300 g/10 oz. cooked and peeled prawns/shrimp

1 tablespoon finely chopped celery

1 tablespoon finely diced yellow or red (bell) pepper

½ iceberg lettuce, shredded

chopped fresh chives, to garnish

Serves 8

Cut a small cross in the base of each tomato. Place in an airtight container with the vodka, Worcestershire and Tabasco sauce, cover and marinate in the fridge for at least 6 hours, or ideally overnight.

Slice each marinated tomato in half and set aside.

Put the mayonnaise and tomato purée/paste in a large mixing bowl and stir to combine. Fold in the prawns/shrimp, tomatoes, celery and (bell) pepper.

Layer the shredded lettuce in serving glasses. Top each with the prawn/shrimp and tomato mixture, garnish with chives and serve at once.

Sun-dried tomato Parmesan spirals

The soft crumbly pastry and the savoury richness of the sun-dried tomato paste is an appetizing combination. Serve with drinks at a party or as a pre-dinner nibble.

125 g/1 cup plain/all-purpose flour

a pinch of salt

75 g/5 tablespoons butter, diced

15 g/¼ cup finely grated Parmesan cheese

1 egg yolk

8 sun-dried tomatoes in oil, plus 1 tablespoon of the oil

a large baking sheet, greased

Makes about 26

First make the pastry. Blend together the flour, salt, butter and Parmesan cheese in a food processor until well combined. Add the egg yolk and 1 tablespoon of cold water, and blend until the mixture comes together to form a ball. Transfer to a lightly oiled mixing bowl, cover and chill in the fridge for 1 hour.

Meanwhile, blend together the tomatoes with a tablespoon of their oil to form a paste.

Preheat the oven to 200°C (400°F) Gas 6.

Divide the chilled pastry into two equal parts and roll out thinly on a lightly floured surface to make a two rectangles about 16 x 11 cm (6¼ x 4¼ in.). Spread each with the tomato paste, then carefully roll up the pastry from the longest edge. Slice into 1-cm/⅜-in. thick rounds.

Transfer the rounds to the prepared baking sheet and bake in the preheated oven for 20 minutes until golden. Cool on a wire rack, then serve at once or store in an airtight container.

Pan Catalan

Simple pleasures are the best. This classic Spanish snack goes perfectly with traditional Spanish serrano ham.

10 slices rustic bread

1 garlic clove, peeled

2 ripe, juicy tomatoes (such as Globe), halved

extra virgin olive oil, to taste

a pinch of salt

Makes 20

Begin by toasting the bread slices under a grill/broiler until lightly golden on one side only.

Rub the peeled garlic over the toasted side of each bread slice. Rub the tomatoes cut-side down over the bread in the same way.

Cut each slice in half, drizzle generously with oil and season with a touch of salt. Serve at once.

Smoked mackerel cherry tomatoes

These small filled cherry tomato halves look and taste great. The salty mackerel complements the sweet, yet tangy tomato beautifully.

1 smoked mackerel fillet (about 70 g/2½ oz.), skinned

1 tablespoon creamed horseradish sauce

1 tablespoon crème fraîche or sour cream

freshly ground black pepper

14 cherry tomatoes

finely chopped fresh parsley, to garnish

Makes 28

In a food processor, blend together the smoked mackerel, horseradish sauce and crème fraîche to form a pâté. Season with black pepper. Cover and chill for at least 30 minutes.

Next, prepare the tomatoes. Cut them in half and, using a teaspoon, carefully scoop out the soft pulp and seeds, creating 28 cherry tomato shells.

Fill each shell with the chilled smoked mackerel pâté. Return to the fridge until you are ready to serve. Sprinkle with parsley and serve fridge-cold.

Tuna empanadas

Empanadas are a popular snack in Central and South America. Serve alongside mojito cocktails for a party.

450 g/3½ cups plain/all-purpose flour

2 teaspoons baking powder

1 teaspoon salt

60 g/4 tablespoons each of lard and butter, diced

½ tablespoon olive oil

1 garlic clove, peeled and finely chopped

½ onion, peeled and diced

200 g/6–7 oz. tomatoes, scalded (see page 17), peeled, pulp discarded and shells diced

200 g/6½ oz. canned tuna in oil, drained and flaked

2 tablespoons tomato purée/paste

a pinch of chilli powder

½ teaspoon ground cumin

salt and freshly ground black pepper, to taste

vegetable oil, for frying

a 7.5-cm/3¼-in. cookie cutter

Makes 20

First, make the pastry. Put the flour, baking powder and salt in a large mixing bowl. Add the lard and butter and rub in with your fingertips. Add in 4–6 tablespoons of cold water, a tablespoon at a time, bringing together with a knife to form a soft dough. Wrap in clingfilm/plastic wrap and chill for 1 hour.

Meanwhile, prepare the filling. Heat the olive oil in a frying pan/skillet. Add the garlic and onion and fry until softened. Add the chopped tomato shells and fry for 5 minutes, stirring often. Mix in the tuna, tomato purée/paste, chilli powder and cumin, and season with salt and pepper. Cook for 1–2 minutes.

Roll out the pastry on a lightly floured surface and cut out 20 circles using the cookie cutter. Place a teaspoon of the filling in the centre of each pastry circle, brush the edges with water and fold over, pressing together to form little pasties.

Heat the vegetable oil in a large frying pan/skillet. Fry the empanadas until lightly browned on all sides. Remove from the oil using a slotted spoon, drain on paper towels and serve.

Tomato basil granita

Granitas, with their distinctive rough texture, are gloriously refreshing treats. Sweet tomatoes and fragrant basil are a classic combination, which work well in this icy form. Serve this pretty pink granita as a refreshing end to a meal.

700 g/1½ lbs. ripe tomatoes (such as Ramapo)

100 g/½ cup caster/ superfine sugar

freshly squeezed juice of ½ lemon

a generous handful of fresh basil leaves

Serves 6

Begin by scalding the tomatoes. Pour boiling water over the ripe tomatoes in a heatproof bowl. Set aside for 1 minute, then drain and carefully peel off the skin using a sharp knife.

Transfer the peeled tomatoes to a food processor and blend to a purée. Add the sugar and lemon juice and blend again briefly to mix in. Shred the basil leaves and stir through the mixture.

Transfer the tomato mixture to an airtight container, cover and freeze for 2 hours. Remove from the freezer and, using a fork, scrape the frozen part of the mixture from around the edges of the container, mixing it in with the unfrozen part. Freeze for a further hour, then repeat the scraping and mixing process. Freeze for a further hour, stir and serve.

Tomato mousse

With its delicate flavour and smooth texture, this mousse makes an elegant appetizer for a summer dinner party.

1 tablespoon olive oil

1 shallot, peeled and finely chopped

1 sprig of fresh thyme

800 g/1¾ lbs. ripe tomatoes, scalded (see left), peeled and diced

1 roasted red (bell) pepper

6 sheets leaf gelatine, soaked and squeezed

200 ml/¾ cup double/ heavy cream

salt and freshly ground black pepper, to taste

4 yellow or red cherry tomatoes, halved, deseeded and diced

8 fresh basil leaves, shredded

6 ramekins, lightly oiled

Serves 6

Heat the oil in a heavy-bottomed saucepan or pot set over a low heat. Add the shallot and thyme and cook until softened. Add the tomatoes, cover and cook for 5 minutes. Uncover and stir well to break down the tomatoes. Add the roasted (bell) pepper and cook for 5 minutes. Season well, blend to a purée and set aside to cool.

Heat a little of the cooled purée in a small pan set over a medium heat, until just below boiling point. Remove from the direct heat and stir in the soaked gelatine until melted. Mix the gelatine mixture into the purée and cool completely.

Whip the cream in a large bowl to soft peaks. Gently fold in the cooled tomato purée. Divide the mixture between the prepared ramekins and chill in the fridge for around 4 hours, until set.

Toss together the cherry tomatoes and basil and top each tomato mousse before serving at once.

Tomato blinis

These little orange-coloured pancakes look appealing and taste good, too! They make the perfect canapé.

110 g/1 scant cup plain/all-purpose flour

½ teaspoon fast-action dried yeast

½ teaspoon white sugar

½ teaspoon salt

150 ml/⅔ cup warm whole milk

1 egg, separated

20 g/4 teaspoons butter, melted

1 tablespoon double concentrate tomato purée/paste

sour cream, Parma ham and chopped fresh chives, to serve

Makes about 26

Begin by making the batter. Sift the flour into a warm mixing bowl. Stir in the yeast, sugar and salt. Whisk the warm milk into the flour mixture to form a thick batter. Whisk in the egg yolk, melted butter and tomato purée/paste. Cover and set aside in warm place to rise for 1 hour.

Preheat the oven to 110°C (225°F) Gas ¼.

In a separate bowl, whisk the egg white to stiff peaks. Gently fold the whisked egg white into the risen batter.

Set a large, heavy-bottomed non-stick frying pan/skillet over medium heat. Carefully drop tablespoonfuls of the batter into the pan, well spaced apart. Fry until tiny bubbles appear on the surface of each blini and the edges darken, then turn over and briefly and lightly brown the other side. Transfer to a baking sheet and keep warm in the preheated oven. Cook the remaining batter in batches until it is all used up.

When ready to serve, top each blini with a little sour cream, a small piece of Parma ham and chopped chives.

Plum tomato tartlets

Dainty, subtly flavourful tartlets make a sophisticated snack for a drinks party.

150 g/1 cup plus 3 tablespoons plain/ all-purpose flour

a pinch of salt

75 g/5 tablespoons butter

3 egg yolks

200 ml/scant 1 cup crème fraîche or sour cream

salt and freshly ground black pepper

2 tablespoons chopped fresh tarragon leaves, plus extra to garnish

100 g/3 oz. soft goat's cheese, chopped

12 baby plum tomatoes (such as San Marzano 2 or Italian Pompeii), halved lengthways

a 4-cm/1½-in. cookie cutter

2 x 12-hole muffin pans, oiled

Makes 24

First make the pastry. Blend together the flour, salt and butter in a food processor until well combined. Add 1 egg yolk and 1 tablespoon of cold water, and blend until the mixture comes together to form a ball. Wrap in clingfilm/plastic wrap and chill in the fridge for at least 30 minutes.

Preheat the oven to 200°C (400°F) Gas 6.

Roll the pastry out thinly on a lightly floured surface and cut out 24 rounds using the cookie cutter. Line the muffin pans with the pastry.

To make the filling, whisk the crème fraîche and the remaining egg yolks together in a jug/pitcher. Season with salt and pepper and add the tarragon.

Divide the goat's cheese evenly between the pastry cases, then nestle in two halved plum tomatoes in each case, skin side-down. Carefully pour in a little of the crème fraîche mixture, then bake in the preheated oven for 30 minutes until the filling has risen and is golden.

Garnish with tarragon, if desired, and serve warm.

Varieties and handling

One of the wonderful things about the tomato is the huge range available; there are literally hundreds of different tomato varieties. Tomatoes range enormously in size – from tiny cherry tomatoes to huge beefsteak tomatoes – and also shape; think sphere, plum and heart, smooth, ridged, irregular. While red is the colour primarily associated with tomatoes, they also come in hues including yellow, orange, green, pink and purple-black and also striped or patched with colour. It is not just their appearance that varies, but also their flavour and texture: sweet, acidic, juicy or dry-textured, firm-fleshed or soft. The range of tastes available is fascinating; the Black Russian tomato, for example, has a noticeably smoky taste, reminiscent of smoked bacon. Increasingly, a larger range of varieties are on offer in grocers, farmers' markets and supermarkets, offering the tomato enthusiast the chance to explore this vegetable fruit in all its glorious diversity.

While tomatoes overall are remarkably versatile, able to be used in many different ways, different varieties have distinctive characteristics. 'Classic tomatoes' is the term used to describe the medium-sized, round tomatoes we are most familiar with. These everyday tomatoes can be eaten both raw and used in cooking and are simply called 'tomatoes' within the recipes here.

Plum tomatoes have a distinctive oval shape. Their flesh is noticeably firm and they are drier in the centre than classic tomatoes, so fresh plum tomatoes are often used for toppings on dishes such as savoury tarts or pizzas. They also lend themselves to processing, so can be canned and used to make tomato purée/paste. Good-quality canned plum tomatoes are a very useful store-cupboard staple.

One striking group of tomatoes is the beefsteak, which can grow to an impressive size, with a single tomato weighing over 450 g/16 oz.

As the name suggests, this is a meaty, firm-textured tomato, lending itself to slicing. One of the most famous of the beefsteak tomatoes is the French Marmande, a large, ribbed tomato which is a speciality originally from the town of Marmande, famed for its tomato cultivation. With its thin skin and few seeds, Marmande tomatoes are excellent in salads, while their large size also lends them to stuffing and baking. In Italy, the large *cuor di bue* (which translates as 'oxheart', or *couer-de-boeuf* in French) tomato is valued for its flavour and firm flesh. It is, indeed, shaped like an oxheart and is ideal in salads such as Insalata Tricolore, served with avocado, mozzarella and fresh basil. Brandywine tomatoes are like the beefsteak but can grow to a much bigger size (a single tomato weighing as much as 700 g/1$\frac{1}{2}$ lbs.) and are pinker in colour and sweeter in taste.

Cherry tomatoes and cocktail tomatoes are easily recognized, since both are much smaller than classic tomatoes. These little tomatoes are characterized by their full, concentrated tomato flavour and are also often noticeably sweet. As they can be eaten whole, their handy snackability makes them an excellent addition to lunch boxes or picnic baskets, either on their own or in salads. When it comes to cooking with them, their small size means that they can be cooked whole, so preserving their shape, making them a pleasantly juicy addition to dishes like macaroni cheese or breads such as focaccia.

Nowadays, many varieties of tomatoes are sold as 'vine' or 'truss' tomatoes, still attached to the stem on which they grew. 'Vine-ripened' tomatoes is the term used to describe tomatoes that have been allowed to ripen on their stems before being harvested, rather than being picked while unripe.

When it comes to cooking with tomatoes, there are two simple techniques which are very useful to know. Many tomato recipes require the soft,

juicy flesh of a ripe tomato, minus the tough skin. Thankfully, skinning ripe tomatoes is very quick and easy to do. Pour boiling water over the ripe tomatoes in a heatproof bowl. Set aside for 1 minute, then drain. Once cool enough to handle, simply pop them out of their skins, making a little cut if needed to help them come out. While it may sound fiddly, it's actually very simple and I find it one of those satisfying kitchen rituals. Do wear an apron though, as very juicy tomatoes can burst when skinned, resulting in a spray of tomato juice and seeds!

Other tomato recipes, those which require the firm flesh of the tomatoes but not its soft juicy seeds, ask for tomatoes to be deseeded. Again,

this is simple to do. Using a small, sharp knife, slice the tomatoes in half across the middle. With the tip of the knife, gently slice the centre of the tomato, cutting the pulp free from the sides, while taking care not to cut through to the shell. Using a small spoon, carefully scoop out the soft seeds and the pulp, creating firm-fleshed tomato shells.

When it comes to storing fresh tomatoes, it Is recommended to store them at room temperature rather than in the fridge, as this allows them to continue to ripen in the ambient temperature. When making a tomato salad, if you do store them in the fridge, make sure to bring fridge-cold tomatoes up to room temperature to enhance their flavour and aroma.

Cherry tomato bruschetta

Juicy tomatoes contrast nicely with the crunchiness of the baked bread in this vibrant, classic Italian snack. Serve as a rustic start to a meal, a midday snack or lunchtime treat.

1 slender baguette

2 teaspoons olive oil

12 red and yellow cherry tomatoes, quartered

1 teaspoon balsamic vinegar

a pinch of salt

1 garlic clove, peeled

4–6 fresh basil leaves, plus extra to garnish

freshly ground black pepper

Makes about 12

Preheat the oven to 200°C (400°F) Gas 6.

Slice the baguette into 1-cm/³/₈-in. thick slices. Transfer to a baking sheet and lightly brush with 1 teaspoon of the oil. Bake in the preheated oven for 20 minutes, until pale gold and crisp. Remove from the oven and set aside to cool.

Meanwhile, mix together the cherry tomato quarters with the remaining olive oil, balsamic vinegar, salt and whole garlic clove in a large bowl. Shred the basil leaves and mix in. Set aside to allow the flavours to infuse while the baguette slices bake and cool.

Discard the garlic clove from the tomato mixture, then spoon onto each slice of bread. Garnish with basil leaves and sprinkle with pepper. Serve at once.

Tomato ketchup

Making your own tomato ketchup is both simple and very satisfying. This recipe has a delicious tang and spicy notes. Use it to add relish to dishes such as home-made burgers or these tasty fried green tomatoes.

1 teaspoon celery seeds

3 whole cloves

1 dried red chilli/hot red pepper

1 star anise

600 ml/2½ cups passata/ strained tomatoes (see page 149)

75 ml/⅓ cup white wine vinegar

50 g/¼ cup soft brown sugar

¼ teaspoon mustard powder

1 teaspoon salt

½ teaspoon ground ginger

sterilized glass bottles

Makes about 750 ml/1¼ pints

Wrap the celery seeds, cloves, dried chilli/hot red pepper and star anise in a small piece of muslin/ cheesecloth, forming a spice bag.

Place the passata/strained tomatoes, vinegar, sugar, spice bag, mustard powder, salt and ground ginger in a heavy-bottomed non-reactive pan set over a low heat. Warm gently, stirring until the sugar has dissolved. Turn up the heat and bring to a simmer. Simmer uncovered for 30–40 minutes, stirring now and then, until reduced and thickened. Remove the spice bag and discard. Decant the ketchup into warm, sterilized glass bottles and store in the fridge for up to 12 months.

Fried green tomatoes

A classic American brunch dish, the fresh juiciness of the tomatoes works nicely with their crunchy coating here. Serve with fried bacon and eggs for brunch, or as a side dish.

4 green tomatoes

3 tablespoons fine cornmeal

salt and freshly ground black pepper

the leaves from 1 sprig of fresh thyme, plus extra to garnish

15 g/1 tablespoon butter

2 teaspoons olive oil

1 egg, beaten

seasoned crème fraîche or sour cream, to serve

tomato ketchup (see left), to serve

Serves 4

Slice each tomato into 3–4 even-sized thick slices.

Season the cornmeal with salt and pepper, adding in the thyme leaves, if using. Set aside.

Heat the butter and oil in a heavy-bottomed frying pan/skillet until it begins to froth.

Meanwhile, dip the tomato slices first in the beaten egg, then in the cornmeal mixture, lightly coating them on both sides.

Add the coated tomato slices to the hot pan and fry for 2–3 minutes. Turn them over and fry until golden on both sides.

Serve at once, garnished with thyme, with a dollop of seasoned crème fraîche or sour cream and tomato ketchup on the side.

Patatas bravas

Fried potatoes in a spicy tomato sauce is a popular and traditional Spanish tapas dish. Serve with good-quality cured ham, such as jamón serrano or Parma ham, and a glass of chilled fino Sherry as an appetizing first course.

300 g/10 oz. waxy potatoes, peeled

2 tablespoons olive oil

1 shallot, peeled and chopped

1 garlic clove, peeled and chopped

1 dried chilli/hot red pepper

1 tablespoon Sherry vinegar

400 g/14 oz. canned plum tomatoes

salt and freshly ground black pepper

1 teaspoon hot smoked paprika/pimentón

chopped fresh parsley, to garnish

Serves 4

Boil the potatoes in salted boiling water until just tender; drain, cool and dice.

Meanwhile, prepare the spicy tomato sauce. Heat 1 tablespoon of the oil in a small, heavy-bottomed frying pan/skillet. Add the shallot and garlic and crumble in the dried chilli/hot red pepper. Fry, stirring, for 1–2 minutes until fragrant. Add the Sherry vinegar and continue to cook for 1 minute, until syrupy. Add the canned tomatoes and mix well. Season with salt, pepper and the smoked paprika/pimentón. Turn up the heat and bring to the boil. Cook the sauce uncovered, stirring often to break down the tomatoes, for 10–15 minutes, until reduced and thickened.

In a separate large frying pan/skillet, heat the remaining olive oil. Add the cooled, diced potatoes and fry until golden brown on all sides, stirring often and seasoning with salt. Pour the cooked tomato sauce over the potatoes, garnish with parsley and serve hot or at room temperature.

soups and salads

Pappa al pomodoro

A classic Tuscan dish, pappa al pomodoro is based, with characteristic frugality, on simple ingredients – dry bread, ripe tomatoes, olive oil and fragrant basil – transformed into a flavourful, thick-textured 'soup'. As with all Italian cuisine, using quality ingredients is key, so choose good bread, the juiciest of tomatoes and a fine extra virgin olive oil.

250 g/8 oz. day-old sourdough bread

1 kg/2¼ lbs. ripe tomatoes

2 tablespoons olive oil

2 garlic cloves, peeled and crushed

salt and freshly ground black pepper

150 ml/⅔ cup tomato passata/strained tomatoes (see page 149)

150 ml/⅔ cup hot water

leaves from a small bunch of fresh basil

2 tablespoons extra virgin olive oil, plus extra to serve

Serves 4–6

Preheat the oven to 100°C (215°F) Gas ¼.

Slice the bread thickly and trim off the crusts. Place the bread in the oven for 15–20 minutes in order to dry it out, then set aside.

Next, scald the tomatoes. Pour boiling water over the ripe tomatoes in a heatproof bowl. Set aside for 1 minute, then drain and carefully peel off the skin using a sharp knife. Roughly chop, reserving any juices, and set aside.

Heat the olive oil in a large, heavy-bottomed saucepan or pot set over a medium heat. Add the garlic and fry gently, stirring continuously for 2 minutes, until fragrant. Add the chopped tomatoes with their juices, stir and season with salt and pepper. Bring the mixture to the boil, reduce the heat and simmer uncovered for 30 minutes, stirring now and then to break down the tomatoes. Add the tomato passata/strained tomatoes and hot water, mix well and simmer for a couple of minutes.

Tear the dried bread into small pieces and mix into the tomato soup, so that it thickens, resembling porridge in texture. Mix in the basil leaves and extra virgin olive oil.

Serve with a drizzle of extra virgin olive oil over each serving.

Thai gazpacho

This Southeast Asian take on a classic Spanish gazpacho is a wonderfully refreshing dish, perfect for summer entertaining. For optimum flavour, choose the ripest, tastiest tomatoes you can find.

700 g/1½ lbs. ripe tomatoes

2 lemon grass stalks

1 garlic clove, peeled

1 red onion, peeled and chopped

a 5-cm/2-In. piece of fresh ginger, peeled and chopped

150 ml/²/₃ cup tomato juice

2 tablespoons rice or white wine vinegar

2 tablespoons olive oil

salt and freshly ground black pepper

6 kaffir lime leaves

1 red (bell) pepper, deseeded and finely diced

¼ cucumber, finely diced

Serves 4

Begin by scalding the tomatoes. Pour boiling water over the ripe tomatoes in a heatproof bowl. Set aside for 1 minute, then drain and carefully peel off the skin using a sharp knife. Set aside.

Peel the tough outer casing from the lemon grass stalks. Finely chop the white, lower, bulbous part of each stalk, discarding the remaining fibrous stalk.

In a food processor, blend the peeled tomatoes, lemon grass, garlic, onion, ginger, tomato juice, vinegar and oil until finely chopped. Transfer the mixture to a large jug/pitcher. Stir in 150 ml/²/₃ cup of water and season with salt and pepper.

Tear the kaffir lime leaves into shreds, discarding the central vein, and mix into the gazpacho. Cover and chill in the fridge for at least 4 hours.

To serve, pour the gazpacho into bowls and garnish with diced (bell) pepper and cucumber.

Green tomato and sorrel soup

Tangy green tomatoes and lemon-flavoured sorrel combine to make a deliciously refreshing and sophisticated-tasting cold soup. If you can't source fresh sorrel, leaf spinach with a squeeze of lemon juice makes a tasty alternative. Serve as an appetizer or light lunch with bread and butter on the side.

50 g/2 cups sorrel leaves

25 g/2 tablespoons butter

1 shallot, finely chopped

500 g/1 lb. green tomatoes, roughly chopped

600 ml/2½ cups chicken or vegetable stock

salt and freshly ground black pepper

4 tablespoon plain yogurt, to garnish

Serves 4

First, prepare the sorrel. Tear the leaves off the tough ribs and shred the leaves finely.

Melt the butter in a heavy-bottomed saucepan or pot set over a medium heat. Add the shallot and fry gently for 2–3 minutes until softened, stirring now and then. Add the tomatoes and shredded sorrel and continue to cook, stirring often, for 2–3 minutes.

Add the stock to the pan, stir to combine and season with salt and pepper. Bring to the boil, reduce the heat, cover and simmer for 25 minutes.

Blend the soup until smooth, then strain through a fine mesh sieve/strainer set over a jug/pitcher. Cool completely, then chill in the fridge for at least 2 hours.

Serve each portion garnished with a swirl of plain yogurt and seasoned with pepper.

Tomato and roast squash soup

This vibrant soup combines the natural sweetness of roasted butternut squash with the bright acidity of fresh tomatoes to create an appealing vegetable soup. Serve with crusty bread on the side.

300 g/10 oz. butternut squash, peeled and diced into 1-cm/³/₈-in. cubes

1¹/₂ tablespoons olive oil

salt and freshly ground black pepper

800 g/1³/₄ lbs. ripe tomatoes

1 onion, peeled and chopped

1 garlic clove, peeled and chopped

2 sprigs of fresh thyme

grated zest and freshly squeezed juice of 1 orange

300 ml/1¹/₄ cups chicken or vegetable stock

Serves 4

Preheat the oven to 200°C (400°F) Gas 6.

Toss the squash with ¹/₂ tablespoon of the oil in a roasting pan. Season with salt and pepper, and roast in the preheated oven for 25 minutes until softened.

Meanwhile, scald the tomatoes. Pour boiling water over the ripe tomatoes in a heatproof bowl. Set aside for 1 minute, then drain and carefully peel off the skin using a sharp knife. Roughly chop, reserving any juices, and set aside.

Heat the remaining tablespoon of oil in a large saucepan or pot set over a low heat. Add the onion, garlic and thyme and fry gently for 3–5 minutes, stirring often, until softened and fragrant. Add the chopped tomatoes, together with their juices, and the orange zest and juice. Increase the heat, cover and cook for 5 minutes, bringing to the boil.

Uncover and cook for a further 10 minutes, stirring often, to break down the tomatoes. Add the stock and season with salt and pepper. Bring the mixture to the boil, reduce the heat and simmer for 15 minutes. Add in the roasted squash, simmer for a final 5 minutes to heat through, then serve immediately.

Grow your own

Growing your own tomatoes is relatively easy to do and is very rewarding when you harvest and enjoy the results. Picking plump, sun-warm, ripe, home-grown tomatoes from their stems, releasing that wonderful tomato scent as your hand brushes the leaves, is a simple but satisfying pleasure, as, indeed, is eating them!

Tomatoes need warm, sheltered conditions in order to do well. For the best crops, growing tomatoes in a greenhouse or under a growing frame is ideal. However, tomato plants can be grown outside, although they will require a sunny, well-sheltered spot in order to flourish. First of all,

check that the varieties you plant are suitable for outdoor growing. Be sure, also, to wait for the weather to warm up sufficiently before venturing to plant them outside, as tomato plants dislike the cold and will simply stop growing if exposed to cold weather.

Such is the tomato's popularity that there is a huge range of varieties to choose from. Broadly speaking, tomatoes are divided into two major types, based on how they grow: vine (also known as 'cordon') or bush. Each of these types have different requirements when it comes to looking after them.

Growing well in greenhouses, vine tomatoes grow upwards, producing tomatoes on trusses hanging from the main stem. They require staking up in order to support them. This is simply done by pushing a long stake (wooden and metal rods both work well) into the soil near each seedling and loosely tying the main stem to the stake with garden twine as it grows. In order to produce a good crop, it is important to pinch out the unwanted side-shoots that appear between the leaf stems and the main stem on vine tomatoes. Once a vine tomato plant has produced four or five flower trusses, it is recommended that you pick out the growing tip in order to prevent it growing more; this way, the plant's energy goes into the actual tomatoes.

Bush tomato plants, which grow tomatoes from side branches, lend themselves to outdoor planting and are good for grow bags. Some varieties can be grown in hanging baskets or deep window boxes. They require much less attention than vine tomatoes and there is no need to support them with stakes. A mulch of straw around bush tomato plants is recommended, as this prevents the tomatoes from trailing on the ground and helps protect them from being eaten by slugs and snails.

Growing your own plants from seed (which needs to be done indoors or a greenhouse or in a heated propagator for the early stages) offers you a far greater choice of varieties, including the chance to grow more unusual heirloom varieties of tomato. Plant the seeds in seed trays filled with multi-purpose potting compost, sowing thinly and covering the seeds with a thin layer of sieved potting compost. Once they have grown their first pair of leaves, carefully prick out the seedlings and transfer them into individual pots. Grow them in a warm, bright place with good ventilation. Alternately, buy tomato seedlings from garden centres and plant up into larger pots, grow-bags or directly into soil. Tomatoes require a lot of nutrients, so be sure to use soil enriched with well-rotted garden compost. Take care to disturb the soil around the roots as little as possible when planting out and always generously water the plants when first setting them out.

Tomatoes need frequent and regular watering in order to flourish and thrive, with the aim being to keep the soil and roots evenly moist. If the plants are allowed to dry out, this can lead to them splitting. Using a mulch around the plants is a simple but effective way of retaining moisture in the soil. On the other hand, be aware that over-watering will lead to the plants producing leaves at the expense of fruit and also result in tomatoes that lack an intensity of flavour. Feeding your tomato plants is also important. Once the flowers appear, feed them once a week with a high-potash tomato fertilizer. This will boost flowering and fruiting.

Tomatoes ripen and are ready for harvesting from midsummer onwards. When it comes to picking them, choose tomatoes that have coloured evenly. Ideally, leave them growing until they have fully ripened so that you eat them at their very best. To encourage ripening if the season is drawing to an end and the weather is turning cold, cover bush tomato plants with a garden cloche or fleece. Bear in mind that unripe green tomatoes can be used for cooking in dishes such as the Fried Green Tomatoes on page 24 or the Green Tomato Chutney on page 155.

If you yield a glut of tomatoes that can't be used right away, freeze them whole. Handily, frozen tomatoes can be skinned by simply running a frozen tomato under cold water, with the result that the skin then slips off. The tomato flesh tends to soften after freezing but can be used to make soups or sauces – the options are endless.

Tomato, freekeh & avocado

Freekeh's slightly chewy texture and nutty flavour contrasts
nicely with the tomato and avocado in this simple, Middle
Eastern–inspired salad. Serve as part of a buffet meal or
as a side dish to cold roast chicken.

100 g/²/₃ cup freekeh (a cracked, roasted
  green wheat)

1 ripe avocado

freshly squeezed juice of ½ lemon

12 cherry tomatoes, quartered

2 sun-dried tomatoes in oil, chopped

1 spring onion/scallion, finely chopped

2 tablespoons argan oil (or walnut oil)

2 tablespoons finely chopped fresh parsley

1 tablespoon pine nuts, toasted

Serves 4

Cook the freekeh in a pan of boiling, salted water, simmering for 15–20 minutes
until tender. Drain and allow to cool.

Using a sharp knife, cut the avocado in half, turning it as you do to cut around
the stone/pit. Twist the two halves to separate. Remove the stone/pit and peel
the two halves. Dice the flesh and toss with a little of the lemon juice to prevent
any discolouration.

Mix together the cooked freekeh, cherry tomatoes, sun-dried tomatoes
and spring onion/scallion. Toss with the oil, the remaining lemon juice and
parsley. Fold in the diced avocado, top with pine nuts and serve at once.

Heritage tomato fennel salad

Good, fresh tomatoes need little else to showcase them. Choose the best, varied tomatoes you can find and enjoy them, simply.

15 g/2 tablespoons flaked/slivered almonds

1 large fennel bulb

6–8 heritage tomatoes, ideally in assorted varieties

3 tablespoons extra virgin olive oil

1 tablespoon freshly squeezed lemon juice

1 teaspoon sweet smoked paprika/pimentón

salt and freshly ground black pepper

Serves 4

Toast the flaked/slivered almonds in a small, dry heavy-bottomed frying pan/skillet until golden-brown. Swirl the pan regularly so that they don't burn. Remove from the pan and set aside.

Trim the fennel bulb, reserving the fronds, and slice very finely. Cut the tomatoes into thin slices.

Mix together the oil, lemon juice and smoked paprika/pimentón to make a dressing, seasoning with salt and pepper.

Arrange the fennel and tomato slices on a serving plate. Lightly toss with the dressing, sprinkle over the toasted almonds, garnish with the reserved fennel fronds and serve at once.

Panzanella

Perfect for a summertime lunch, this is a classic, rustic Tuscan recipe. Traditionally, it was made frugally with stale bread, given new life by being mixed with fresh tomatoes and flavourful olive oil. For best results, choose the ripest tomatoes that you can find.

1 red onion, peeled and very finely sliced into rings

100 ml/6 tablespoons white wine vinegar

2 teaspoons sugar

½ teaspoon salt

1 large yellow or red (bell) pepper

200 g/6½ oz. day-old rustic bread

500 g/1 lb. ripe tomatoes, ideally in assorted colours and shapes

100 ml/6 tablespoons extra virgin olive oil

50 ml/3 tablespoons red wine vinegar

1 garlic clove, peeled and crushed (optional)

1 teaspoon capers, rinsed

salt and freshly ground black pepper, to taste

a generous handful of fresh basil leaves

Serves 6–8

First, lightly pickle the onion rings. Place them in a colander and pour over freshly boiled water. Transfer the onion rings to a mixing bowl and add the vinegar, sugar and salt. Pour over 150 ml/²⁄₃ cup of water and mix together. Set aside for 1 hour, drain and dry on paper towels.

Meanwhile, grill/broil the (bell) pepper under a medium heat until charred on all sides. Place in a plastic bag (as trapping the steam makes the pepper easier to peel) and set aside to cool. Peel using a sharp knife and cut into short, thick strips.

Trim and discard the crusts from the bread and slice into small cubes. Cut the tomatoes into chunks or in half if using small cherry tomatoes.

Make the dressing by mixing together the oil, red wine vinegar, garlic and capers. Season with salt and pepper, bearing in mind the saltiness of the capers.

Mix together the chopped tomatoes, bread and roasted pepper strips in a large serving bowl. Pour the dressing over the mixture and toss together, ensuring all the ingredients are well coated. Add the pickled onion rings, then the basil. Mix well and set aside for 15–20 minutes to allow the flavours to infuse before serving.

Tomato tabbouleh

This zingy tomato and parsley salad is a Lebanese classic, traditionally served as a mezze dish. Gloriously refreshing, it goes well with grilled fish, chicken or lamb.

1 tablespoon bulgur wheat

350 g/12 oz. ripe but firm tomatoes

100 g/1 cup fresh flat-leaf parsley

1 spring onion/scallion, finely chopped

2 tablespoons finely sliced mint leaves

freshly squeezed juice of 1 lemon

2 tablespoons extra virgin olive oil

salt and freshly ground black pepper

fresh mint sprigs, to garnish

Serves 4

Soak the bulgur wheat in cold water for 15 minutes to soften.

Meanwhile, finely dice the tomatoes, discarding the white stem base. Trim off and discard the stalks of the flat-leaf parsley and finely chop the leaves. If using a food processor, take care not to over-chop the parsley as it may turn to a pulp; you want the parsley to retain its texture.

Drain the soaked bulgur wheat, squeezing it dry of excess moisture. Toss together the diced tomatoes, chopped parsley, bulgur wheat, spring onion/scallion and mint. Add the lemon juice, oil, season with salt and pepper, and toss well.

Garnish the tabbouleh with mint and serve at once.

Tomato fattoush

Crisp pitta bread contrasted with juicy tomatoes and crunchy cucumber and radishes makes this version of a classic Lebanese mezze dish a salad to relish. Serve for a light meal or as an accompaniment to roasted lamb.

1 pitta bread

2½ tablespoons extra virgin olive oil

500 g/1 lb. tomatoes, sliced thickly

½ cucumber, halved lengthways and sliced

6 radishes, finely sliced

1 spring onion/scallion, finely chopped

freshly squeezed juice of ½ lemon

a pinch of salt

2 tablespoons chopped fresh flat-leaf parsley

2 teaspoons ground sumac

Serves 4

Slice the pitta around its edges to form two thin pitta halves. Brush with ½ tablespoon of the oil and grill/broil under a medium heat for 2–3 minutes until golden-brown and crisp. Cool, then tear into small pieces.

Toss together the tomatoes, cucumber, radishes and spring onion/scallion in a serving bowl.

To make the dressing, mix together the remaining oil and the lemon juice, season with salt and pour over the salad. Mix in the crisp pitta bread pieces and parsley.

Sprinkle with sumac and serve at once.

Thai tomato salad

This Thai-style salad, with its salty-sweet, chilli-flavoured dressing, is easy to put together. Serve it as a pleasingly textured side dish with a rich beef and coconut-milk curry and steamed rice.

16 cherry tomatoes, quartered

200 g/2 cups sugar snap peas, trimmed and halved

1 courgette/zucchini, grated

1 carrot, peeled and grated

2 tablespoons Thai fish sauce

1 tablespoon rice vinegar

2 teaspoons sweet chilli sauce

freshly squeezed juice of ½ lime

50 g/⅓ cup roasted peanuts, finely ground

a handful of fresh Thai basil leaves, to garnish

Serves 4

Toss together the cherry tomatoes, sugar snap peas, courgette/zucchini and carrot in a serving dish.

To make the dressing, mix together the Thai fish sauce, vinegar, sweet chilli sauce and lime juice. Pour over the salad.

Mix in the ground peanuts, garnish with Thai basil leaves and serve at once.

Tomato, melon and feta salad

Perfect food for hot-weather dining. Sweet melon combined with juicy tomatoes and contrasted with salty feta, makes this a lovely dish. For a saltier contrast, substitute the feta with blue cheese and add sliced Parma ham. Serve with crusty bread to mop up every last drop of deliciousness.

½ Galia or other green-fleshed melon, peeled, deseeded and diced

½ cantaloupe melon, peeled, deseeded and diced

300 g/10 oz. tomatoes, sliced into wedges

2 tablespoons extra virgin olive oil

1 tablespoon Sherry vinegar

2 tablespoons finely chopped fresh chives

freshly ground black pepper

100 g/3½ oz. feta cheese, diced

Variation

50 g/2 oz. blue cheese, such as Stilton or Gorgonzola, crumbled into pieces

3 slices of Parma ham, shredded

Serves 4

Toss together all the melon and tomato pieces with the oil, vinegar and chives in a serving dish. Season well with pepper.

Gently mix in the feta cheese and serve at once.

Variation
Follow the instructions as above, replacing the feta with blue cheese. Stir in the shredded Parma ham and serve at once.

Kachumber

Piquant green chilli/chile, fragrant cumin, tangy lemon juice and fresh mint combine to give a vibrant kick to this classic, easy-to-make, appealingly textured Indian salad. Serve it as an accompaniment to dishes such as tandoori fish or prawns, or baked or poached salmon.

600 g/1¼ lbs. ripe tomatoes

1 shallot

½ cucumber

2 teaspoon cumin seeds

1 green chilli/chile (such as serrano), deseeded and finely chopped

salt and freshly ground black pepper

a handful of fresh mint leaves, shredded

freshly squeezed juice of ¼ lemon

4 lemon wedges

Serves 4

Begin by scalding the tomatoes. Pour boiling water over the ripe tomatoes in a heatproof bowl. Set aside for 1 minute, then drain and carefully peel off the skin using a sharp knife. Slice the tomatoes in half, scoop out and remove the pulp and slice the tomato shells.

Peel the shallot, slice lengthways and finely slice into semi-circles. Put the shallot slices in a colander and pour over freshly boiled water. Pat dry with paper towels and set aside.

Peel the cucumber, slice in half lengthways and scoop out the seeds. Finely slice and set aside.

Toast the cumin seeds in a small, dry heavy-bottomed frying pan/skillet until fragrant. Swirl the pan regularly so that they don't burn. Remove from the pan and set aside to cool.

Toss together the chopped tomatoes, shallot, cucumber, green chilli/chile and toasted cumin seeds. Season with salt and pepper, add the mint leaves and lemon juice and toss to combine.

Serve at once with a wedge of lemon on the side.

Sun-blush tomato, orange and burrata salad

Gloriously simple to put together, this bright and colourful dish offers a Mediterranean-inspired combination of colours, textures and flavours.

2 large oranges

24 sun-blush/semi-dried cherry tomato halves (see page 153)

2 burrata cheeses (or good-quality fresh mozzarella cheese)

To serve
extra virgin olive oil

freshly ground black pepper

a handful of fresh basil leaves

Serves 4

Peel the oranges, making sure to trim off all the white pith, and cut into even, thick slices.

Place the orange slices on a large serving dish, then scatter over the sun-blush/semi-dried tomato halves. Tear the burrata cheeses into chunks and layer on top of the orange slices.

Drizzle with extra virgin olive oil and season with pepper. Garnish with basil leaves and serve at once.

poultry, meat and fish

Chicken cacciatore

Chicken cacciatore translates as 'hunter's chicken'. Classic Italian ingredients, including tomatoes, garlic and wine, are transformed into a thick, tasty sauce that coats the fried chicken. Serve with mashed potatoes, rice or polenta.

600 g/1¼ lbs. ripe
  tomatoes

4 chicken drumsticks

4 chicken thighs

salt and freshly ground
  black pepper

plain/all-purpose flour,
  to coat

3 tablespoons olive oil

1 rasher/strip of pancetta,
  diced

2 garlic cloves, peeled
  and chopped

4 fresh rosemary sprigs

1 yellow (bell) pepper,
  sliced into strips

75 ml/⅓ cup dry white
  wine

1 tablespoon tomato
  purée/paste

Serves 4

Begin by scalding the tomatoes. Pour boiling water over the ripe tomatoes in a heatproof bowl. Set aside for 1 minute, then drain and carefully peel off the skin using a sharp knife. Roughly chop, reserving any juices, and set aside.

Season the chicken pieces with salt and pepper, then season the flour with salt and pepper in a wide, shallow dish. Coat the chicken pieces in the seasoned flour, ready to fry.

In a large frying pan/skillet, heat 2 tablespoons of the oil. Fry the chicken in batches, until golden-brown on all sides.

Heat the remaining oil in a casserole dish. Add the pancetta and garlic and fry, stirring occasionally, for 1–2 minutes, until the garlic is lightly browned. Add the rosemary and the (bell) pepper and fry for 1 minute. Pour in the wine and cook, stirring occasionally, for 1–2 minutes, until the wine has reduced slightly. Add the chopped tomatoes with their juices, cover and cook for 5 minutes, until the sauce has come to the boil. Stir well, to help the tomatoes break down, then stir in the tomato purée/paste. Season with salt and pepper and simmer uncovered for 10 minutes, stirring from time to time.

Add the browned chicken pieces to the tomato sauce. Bring to the boil, reduce the heat and simmer, partly covered, for 20–30 minutes, until the chicken is cooked through.

Honeyed duck and apricot tagine

Duck and dried apricots cooked in a fragrant, fresh tomato sauce make a rich tagine, enriched further with honey. Serve with steamed couscous and green beans.

4 duck legs

1 kg/2¼ lbs. tomatoes

1½ tablespoons olive oil

2 onions, finely chopped

1 cinnamon stick

1 teaspoon ground ginger

1 teaspoon ground coriander

½ teaspoon freshly ground black pepper

salt, to taste

12 dried apricots

a generous pinch of saffron strands, ground and soaked in 1 tablespoon hot water

1 tablespoon clear honey

chopped fresh coriander/cilantro, to garnish

Serves 4

Place the duck legs skin side down in a large, heavy-bottomed frying pan/skillet. Cook gently over a low heat for 10 minutes, so that the fat comes out from the duck legs, then increase the heat and fry until browned on both sides. Season with salt and set aside.

Next, scald the tomatoes. Pour boiling water over the ripe tomatoes in a heatproof bowl. Set aside for 1 minute, then drain and carefully peel off the skin using a sharp knife. Roughly chop, reserving any juices, and set aside.

Heat the oil in a large casserole dish set over a medium heat. Add in the onions and cinnamon and fry for 3 minutes, stirring occasionally, until the onion is softened and fragrant. Mix in the chopped tomatoes, ground ginger, ground coriander and pepper. Season with salt and bring to the boil. Cover and cook for 10 minutes, stirring now and then, so that the tomatoes soften and break down.

Add the browned duck legs to the casserole with the dried apricots and saffron with its soaking liquid. Bring to the boil, cover, reduce the heat and simmer for 1 hour until the duck is tender.

Stir in the honey, sprinkle with chopped fresh coriander/cilantro and serve at once.

Tomato bacon gratin

Juicy, naturally sweet tomatoes and salty bacon are one of those great flavour combinations. Serve this simple-to-make dish for breakfast, brunch or a light lunch, with bread on the side.

1 tablespoon olive oil

2 bacon rashers/slices, finely chopped

1 shallot, peeled and finely chopped

25 g/^{1}/$_{2}$ cup fresh breadcrumbs

a pinch of dried oregano

4 tomatoes

10 g/2^{1}/$_{2}$ tablespoons grated Parmesan cheese

salt and freshly ground black pepper

a shallow ovenproof casserole dish. greased

Serves 4

Preheat the oven to 200°C (400°F) Gas 6.

Heat the oil in a small frying pan/skillet set over a medium heat. Add the bacon and shallot and fry for 2–3 minutes, stirring often, until the shallot has softened and the bacon is cooked. Remove from the heat and stir in the breadcrumbs and oregano.

Slice the tomatoes into 1-cm/^{3}/$_{8}$-in. thick slices. Arrange in the prepared casserole dish, overlapping slightly. Season with a little salt and pepper, bearing in mind the saltiness of the bacon.

Spread the bacon mixture evenly over the tomato slices, then sprinkle over the Parmesan. Bake in the preheated oven for 20 minutes and serve hot from the oven.

Lamb steaks with cherry tomato and anchovy sauce

This tangy sauce, flavoured with savoury anchovies and garlic, is an excellent partner for griddled lamb. Serve with new potatoes and green beans for a simple but satisfying meal.

250 g/½ lb. cherry tomatoes

1 tablespoon olive oil, plus extra for brushing

1 large garlic clove, peeled and sliced

4 anchovy fillets in oil, chopped

4 lamb steaks

salt and freshly ground black pepper

Serves 4

Begin by scalding the tomatoes. Pour boiling water over the ripe tomatoes in a heatproof bowl. Set aside for 1 minute, then drain and carefully peel off the skin using a sharp knife. Slice in half and set aside.

Heat the oil in a small, heavy-bottomed frying pan/skillet set over a low heat. Add the garlic and fry, stirring often, for 1 minute until fragrant. Add the anchovy fillets and continue to fry, stirring continuously, until they melt into the oil. Add the tomato halves and cook, stirring now and then, until the tomatoes have softened to form a sauce. Season with pepper and keep warm until ready to serve.

Preheat a ridged stovetop grill pan over a medium heat.

Season the lamb steaks with salt and pepper, and brush with oil. Cook the lamb steaks in the hot pan as desired.

Serve the grilled steaks with the warm cherry tomato anchovy sauce.

Tomato ginger spare ribs

Spare ribs, braised in an aromatic tomato ginger sauce, make a rich, flavourful dish. Serve with steamed rice and a vegetable side dish, such as blanched Chinese greens.

450 g/1 lb. ripe tomatoes

2 tablespoons oil, plus extra for shallow frying

2 onions, peeled and finely chopped

2 garlic cloves, peeled and chopped

2 x 5-cm/2-in. pieces of fresh ginger, peeled and finely chopped

1 teaspoon Chinese five-spice powder

1 tablespoon Sherry or rice wine

2 teaspoons dark soy sauce

1 tablespoon tomato purée/paste

1 tablespoon brown sugar

300 ml/1¼ cups chicken stock

12 pork spare ribs (about 1.2 kg/2½ lbs.)

Serves 4

Begin by scalding the tomatoes. Pour boiling water over the ripe tomatoes in a heatproof bowl. Set aside for 1 minute, then drain and carefully peel off the skin using a sharp knife. Roughly chop, reserving any juices, and set aside.

Heat the oil in a frying pan/skillet set over a medium heat. Add the onions, garlic and ginger, and fry gently, stirring often, for 2–3 minutes until softened.

Mix the five-spice powder with 1 tablespoon of cold water to form a paste. Add this to the pan with the onions, garlic and ginger, and stir in, frying briefly. Add the Sherry and cook, stirring often, for 1 minute. Add the chopped tomatoes, soy sauce, tomato purée/paste, sugar and chicken stock and mix together. Bring to the boil and cook, stirring occasionally, for 10–15 minutes, until the sauce has thickened and reduced.

Preheat the oven to 200°C (400°F) Gas 6.

Heat enough oil for shallow frying in a large frying pan/skillet set over a medium heat. Cook the spare ribs in batches and brown on all sides. Transfer the ribs to a roasting pan and pour over the tomato sauce to coat.

Bake in the preheated oven for 45 minutes until the ribs are cooked through. Remove and serve hot.

Meatballs in spiced tomato sauce

Fragrant spices enhance the flavour of the tomatoes to make an aromatic sauce for these punchy spiced meatballs. Serve with steamed rice and plain yogurt on the side for a wholesome meal.

500 g/1 lb. tomatoes

2 tablespoons olive oil

1 onion, peeled and chopped

2 garlic cloves, peeled and chopped

a 5-cm/2-in. piece of fresh ginger, peeled and finely chopped

2 cardamom pods

1 cinnamon stick

1 bay leaf

500 g/1 lb. minced/ground lamb or beef

1 teaspoon salt

⅓ teaspoon ground turmeric

2 teaspoons ground cumin

2 teaspoons ground coriander

1 teaspoon freshly ground black pepper

steamed rice, to serve

Serves 4

Begin by scalding the tomatoes. Pour boiling water over the ripe tomatoes in a heatproof bowl. Set aside for 1 minute, then drain and carefully peel off the skin using a sharp knife. Roughly chop, reserving any juices and set aside.

Heat 1 tablespoon of the oil in a large, heavy-bottomed saucepan or casserole dish set over a medium heat. Add the onion, half of the garlic, the ginger, cardamom pods, cinnamon stick and bay leaf. Fry for 1–2 minutes, stirring often, until fragrant. Add the chopped tomatoes with their juices, cover and bring to the boil. Once boiling, uncover and cook for 10 minutes, stirring now and then to break down the tomatoes so that they form a sauce.

Make the meatballs by mixing together the meat, the remaining garlic, salt, ground turmeric, cumin and coriander, and pepper in a large mixing bowl. With wet hands, shape the spiced meat into small meatballs, the size of large marbles.

Heat the remaining oil in a large frying pan/skillet. Add the meatballs and fry, stirring occasionally, until browned on all sides.

Transfer the meatballs to the pan with the tomato sauce and bring to the boil. Reduce the heat, half cover and simmer for 20–25 minutes until the meatballs are cooked through and the sauce has reduced. Serve with steamed rice.

Tomato flavour friends

The tomato's remarkable success as a popular ingredient, widely used around the world, is in large part due to its inherent versatility. Its distinctive yet subtle flavour, combining refreshing acidity with sweetness, goes well with a wide range of ingredients, allowing it to be successfully partnered with them in many diverse dishes. Certain flavour combinations, it must be said, work especially well.

When it comes to herbs that go well with tomatoes, basil leaps to mind as probably the best-known example. With good reason, as the fragrant clove-aniseed-mint notes in basil add a wonderful spicy touch to tomato's bright, clean flavour. In Italian cuisine, where many recipes use

the ripe, flavourful tomatoes that grow so abundantly in Italy, it is noticeable that several of them also feature fresh basil. Classically, of course, there is the salad of juicy, sliced tomatoes, dressed with good olive oil, perhaps enhanced by pieces of soft, moist mozzarella cheese, then topped with freshly torn basil leaves. Sicily's supremely summery version of pesto (see page 149) combines sun-ripened tomatoes with almonds (which grow locally on the island), olive oil and basil. In Naples, pizza is traditionally made by smearing a thin, circular dough base with a tasty tomato sauce, baking it briefly in a hot wood-fired oven, and, for a final flourish, topping it with fresh basil leaves. Use basil to aromatise tomato-based dishes such as soups (hot or cold), sauces, salads, salsas or dressings. Do bear in mind, however, that basil quickly loses its aroma when cooked, so add it in towards the end of the cooking process to maximize its impact.

Another herb that pairs well with tomatoes is tarragon, with its grassy, pine-y anise flavour. The French, for instance, combine fresh tomatoes with herbs including tarragon to create sauce vierge, traditionally served with fish. A simple way of using the two is in a tomato salad, made using chopped tomatoes, layered with lemon slices and a sprinkling of finely chopped tarragon leaves (see recipe on page 81). Feathery dill and delicate chervil are two other herbs that work well with tomatoes. Experiment with sauces, salsas, stuffed tomatoes and soups.

Garlic and tomatoes are another much-loved flavour combination. With its pungent and powerful taste, garlic works well, rooting the tomato in savouriness. Garlic and onion, fried gently in olive oil until softened and mellow, forms the tasty foundation of many classic tomato dishes, such as a tomato sauce to serve with pasta or use on pizza. For a simple and effective way of using the two together, draw inspiration from Catalonia's *pa amb tomàquet*. Served as a popular bar snack, this is made from slices of rough-textured country-style bread rubbed with raw garlic and then juicy fresh tomatoes, so that their juices infuse the bread, finished off with a sprinkling of good quality olive oil.

Ginger is another fundamental flavouring that marries well with tomatoes. One only has to think of the many Indian tomato-based curries that begin by frying onion, garlic and ginger together. The two ingredients combine to be at once aromatic and refreshing, contrasting well with rich meat and poultry such as pork spare ribs, braising beef or duck.

Just as herbs go well with tomatoes, so do spices, adding fragrance and perfume. Saffron, with its distinctive bitter flavour, for example,

is used with tomatoes in French fish soups and stews such as bouillabaisse. Chillies/chiles and tomatoes, which both have their roots in Mexico, are another excellent partnership. Think of flavourful salsas, made from raw tomatoes, which are combined with refreshing citrus elements such as lime or lemon juice to give a tang, and chilli/chile to give a piquant punch. Famous dishes including Singapore's famous chilli crab or drinks like the Bloody Mary use the natural sweetness of tomatoes to mellow the hot chilli/chile kick.

Many salty ingredients work well with tomatoes. The complex saltiness of anchovies is a good example, adding deeper bass notes to tomato's naturally delicate, acidic flavour. Use them to enrich tomato sauces, as with Italy's gutsy puttanesca sauce (see page 126) or fry them gently in oil until they 'melt' before adding tomatoes for hearty stews or braises. Olives work well with tomatoes too; their umami richness contrasts nicely with the freshness of tomato in dishes such as crostini or tarts made with tapenade and tomatoes. Bacon, ham, pancetta and guanciale, again from the same salty umami flavour family, offer much scope for tasty meals, whether in a robust all'Amatriciana sauce or as part of a savoury breakfast, with fried tomatoes nestling alongside slices of ham or bacon.

The tomato's ability to cut through rich ingredients with a zip of acidity makes it an excellent partner with cheese and rich dairy products – try cheese and tomato flans, pasta bakes, toasties or cheese-filled pancakes in a tomato sauce. Vice-versa, a spoonful of double/heavy cream, crème fraîche or natural yogurt stirred into tomato-based dishes such as soups or tomato sauce both enriches and contrasts. For similar reasons, tomatoes are an excellent ingredient to use with pulses, adding a refreshing lift to their characteristic earthy taste. The happy combination can be found around the world, in dishes such as Indian tarka dal, Italian lentil bakes and America's Boston baked beans.

Harissa sardines with tomato salad

A spicy harissa paste adds a pleasant piquant kick to tasty sardines. This is great dish for the barbecue, when the sun is out.

200 g/½ lb. tomatoes

1 red chilli/chile, deseeded and finely chopped

1 garlic clove, peeled and chopped

1 teaspoon caraway seeds

1 tablespoon red wine vinegar

1 teaspoon ground coriander

1 tablespoon olive oil

8 plump fresh sardines, gutted

a pinch of salt

Tomato salad

300 g/10 oz. ripe tomatoes, ideally in assorted colours

1 lemon

extra virgin olive oil, to drizzle

chopped fresh flat-leaf parsley, to serve

freshly ground black pepper, to taste

a large baking sheet, oiled

Serves 4

Begin by scalding the tomatoes. Pour boiling water over the ripe tomatoes in a small pan or pot set over a medium heat. Heat for 1 minute, then remove from the water and carefully peel off the skin using a sharp knife. Roughly chop, reserving the juices.

Blend together the chopped tomatoes with their juices, the chilli/chile, garlic, caraway seeds, vinegar and ground coriander to a paste.

Heat the olive oil in a small frying pan/skillet set over a medium heat. Add the paste and fry, stirring often, for 8–10 minutes, until it thickens and reduces. Season with salt and set aside to cool – you will use this harissa paste to coat the sardines later.

Prepare the tomato salad. Finely slice the tomatoes and the lemon. Arrange the slices in a serving dish, pour over a little extra virgin olive oil. Sprinkle with parsley and season with pepper.

Preheat the grill/broiler to a medium heat.

Cut slashes in the sides of each sardine. Place them on the prepared baking sheet and spread each with the cooled harissa paste on both sides, making sure it gets inside the slashes.

Grill/broil the sardines for 6–10 minutes, until cooked through. Serve at once with the tomato salad on the side.

Greek-style baked fish with tomatoes

Chopped tomatoes give a lovely lift to this simple, easy-to-cook Mediterranean fish dish. Serve with crushed new potatoes and steamed green vegetables.

600 g/1½ lbs. ripe tomatoes

4½ tablespoons olive oil

2 garlic cloves, finely chopped

100 ml/6 tablespoons dry white wine

4 tablespoons chopped fresh flat-leaf parsley, plus extra to garnish

4 white fish steaks (125–150 g/4–5 oz. each)

salt and freshly ground black pepper

a baking dish, greased

Serves 4

Preheat the oven to 200°C (400°F) Gas 6.

Begin by scalding the tomatoes. Pour boiling water over the ripe tomatoes in a heatproof bowl. Set aside for 1 minute, then drain and carefully peel off the skin using a sharp knife. Halve the tomatoes across, scoop out the soft pulp and finely dice the tomato shells.

Heat ½ tablespoon of the oil in a small frying pan/skillet. Add the garlic and fry gently for 1–2 minutes, until softened.

In a bowl, mix together the diced tomato, fried garlic, remaining oil, white wine and parsley.

Season the fish steaks with salt and pepper and place in the prepared baking dish. Spoon the tomato mixture over the fish steaks, then bake in the preheated oven for 20–25 minutes, until the fish is cooked through.

Sprinkle with a little extra chopped parsley and serve at once.

Tuna steaks with miso-glazed tomatoes

The salty savouriness of Japanese miso, combined with sweet, juicy cherry tomatoes, works together really well and makes a delicious garnish for grilled fish such as tuna or swordfish. Serve with plain steamed rice and steamed greens such as gaai laan/kai lan or pak choi/bok choy for a simple yet flavourful meal.

16 cherry tomatoes

4 tuna steaks (125–150 g/ 4–5 oz. each)

salt and freshly ground black pepper

olive oil, for brushing

2 teaspoons brown miso paste

1 tablespoon mirin

1 teaspoon white sugar

½ tablespoon vegetable oil

1 slice of fresh ginger, finely chopped

Serves 4

Begin by scalding the tomatoes. Pour boiling water over the ripe tomatoes in a heatproof bowl. Set aside for 1 minute, then drain, and once cool the tomatoes are cool enough to handle, pop each out of its skin.

Preheat a ridged stovetop grill pan over a medium heat.

Season the tuna with salt and pepper and brush with olive oil. Cook the tuna steaks on the preheated grill pan, until cooked to taste, turning over once.

Meanwhile, mix together the miso paste, mirin and sugar.

Heat the vegetable oil in a small frying pan/skillet. Add the ginger and fry, stirring, for 1 minute, until fragrant. Add the miso mixture, coating the ginger, then add the cherry tomatoes. Fry for 3 minutes, gently stirring the tomatoes to coat them in the sauce without breaking them, until the paste has thickened and reduced.

Serve the tuna steaks with the miso-glazed tomatoes and a little of the miso sauce spooned over them.

Grilled trout fillets with sauce vierge

This uncooked tomato sauce, with its Mediterranean flavours, goes well with the delicate fish. Serve it accompanied by new potatoes for a simple yet elegant meal.

350 g/³⁄₄ lb. ripe tomatoes

I small shallot, peeled and finely chopped

2 tablespoons finely chopped fresh tarragon leaves

2 tablespoons finely chopped fresh flat-leaf parsley

2 tablespoons shredded fresh basil leaves

4 tablespoons extra virgin olive oil

1 tablespoon red wine vinegar

salt and freshly ground black pepper

4 trout fillets (125–150 g/ 4–5 oz. each)

butter, for grilling/broiling

a baking sheet, greased and lined with baking parchment

Serves 4

First, prepare the sauce vierge. Begin by scalding the tomatoes. Pour boiling water over the ripe tomatoes in a heatproof bowl. Set aside for 1 minute, then drain and carefully peel off the skin using a sharp knife. Halve the tomatoes across, scoop out the soft pulp and finely dice the tomato shells.

Mix together the diced tomato, shallot, tarragon, parsley, basil, oil and red wine vinegar. Season with salt and pepper, then set aside for 15 minutes to allow the flavours to meld.

Preheat the grill/broiler to a medium heat.

Place the trout fillets on the prepared baking sheet, season with salt and pepper and dot with a little butter. Grill/broil for 5 minutes until cooked through.

Spoon the sauce vierge over each trout fillet and serve at once.

vegetable dishes

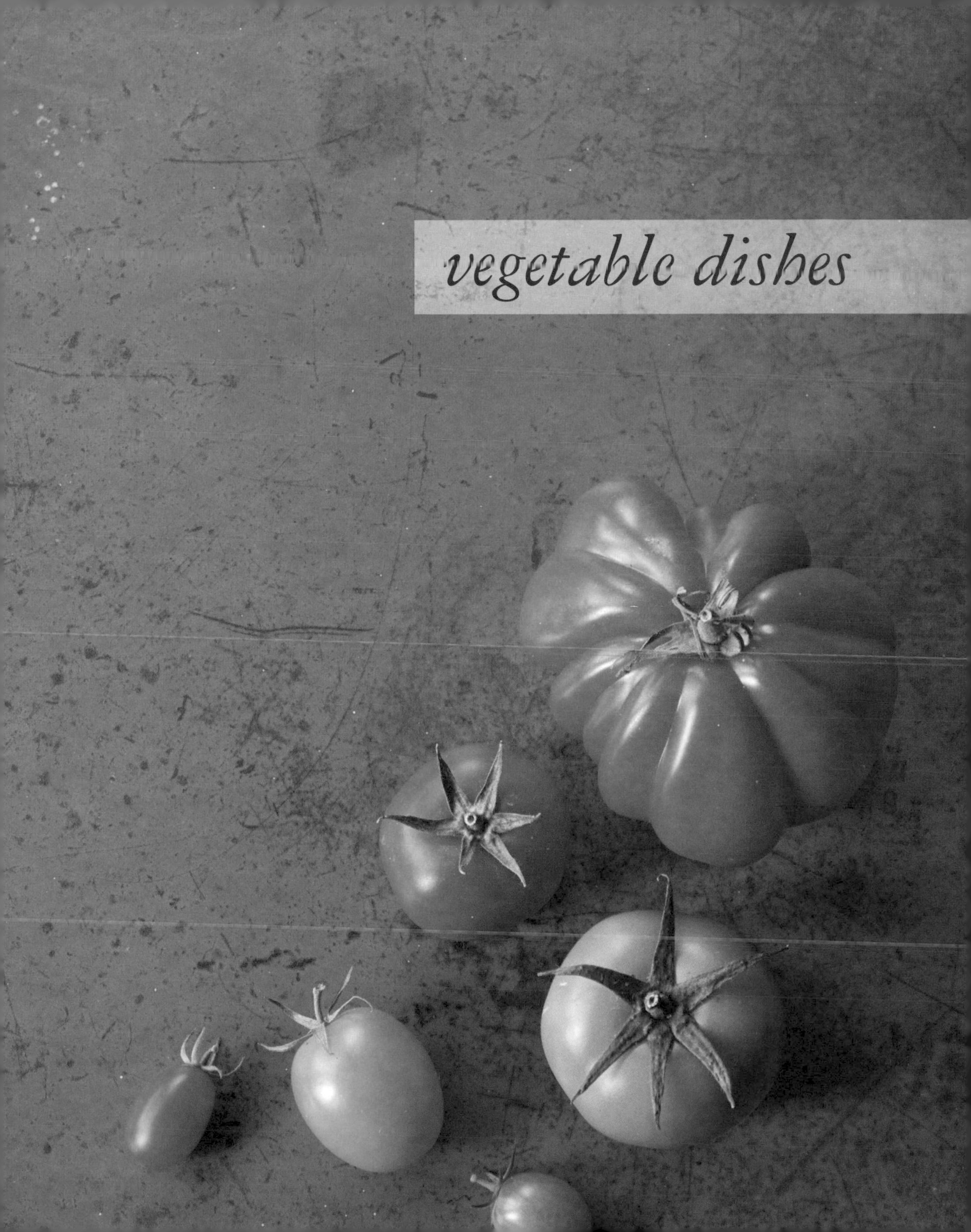

Greek rice-stuffed tomatoes

Evoke summer holidays on Greek islands with this Mediterranean dish, in which a few simple ingredients are transformed into a tasty and satisfying meal.

4–6 large tomatoes

3 tablespoons olive oil

1 small onion, peeled and finely chopped

150 g/¾ cup long grain rice, rinsed

1 teaspoon tomato purée/paste

salt and freshly ground black pepper

2 tablespoons chopped fresh flat-leaf parsley

2 tablespoons chopped fresh dill

2 tablespoons chopped fresh mint

1 teaspoon grated lemon zest

Serves 4

Preheat the oven to 200°C (400°F) Gas 6.

Cut the tops off the tomatoes and carefully scoop out and reserve the soft pulp. Put the tomato shells in a baking dish large enough to hold all tomatoes upright. Set aside with the caps until ready to bake.

Heat 2 tablespoons of the oil in a frying pan/skillet set over a low heat. Add the onion and fry until softened, without allowing it to brown. Add the reserved tomato pulp, the rice and tomato puree/paste. Season well with salt and pepper.

Bring the mixture to the boil and continue to cook for 10 minutes, stirring often. Stir in the parsley, dill, mint and lemon zest.

Fill the tomato shells with the rice mixture and top with their caps. Drizzle with the remaining oil, cover with foil and bake in the preheated oven for 1 hour, until the rice is tender.

Serve warm from the oven or at room temperature.

Tunisian baked eggs in tomato sauce

This classic North African dish makes an excellent brunch dish. Serve it with the Sun-dried tomato and rosemary corn bread on page 134 for mopping up the spiced tomato sauce.

450 g/1 lb. ripe tomatoes

1 tablespoon olive oil

1 onion, peeled and chopped

1 red (bell) pepper, chopped into strips

1 garlic clove, peeled and chopped

1 teaspoon ground cumin

1/2 teaspoon harissa

1 teaspoon brown sugar

salt and freshly ground black pepper

4 eggs

chopped fresh coriander/cilantro, to garnish

Serves 4

Roughly chop the tomatoes, reserving the juices.

Heat the olive oil in a large, heavy-bottomed frying pan/skillet set over a medium heat. Add the onion, (bell) pepper and garlic and fry, stirring often, for 5 minutes, until softened.

Mix together the cumin with 1 tablespoon of water in a small bowl to form a paste.

Add the harissa and cumin paste to the pan and fry, stirring, for a minute. Add the tomatoes and brown sugar, season with salt and pepper, and mix well. Bring to the boil, reduce the heat, cover and simmer for 5 minutes.

Uncover and simmer for a further 10 minutes, stirring now and then, to reduce and thicken the tomato mixture.

Break the eggs, spaced well apart, into the tomato mixture. Cover and cook over a low heat for 10 minutes until the eggs are set.

Sprinkle with coriander/cilantro and serve at once.

Tomatoes in crème fraîche

This simple way of cooking tomatoes transforms them into a tasty dish, with the richness of the crème fraîche contrasting nicely with the natural acidity of the tomatoes. Serve as a side dish with roast lamb or as a light main course with rice or crusty bread.

8 ripe, even-sized tomatoes

1 tablespoon olive oil

1 shallot, finely chopped

1 garlic clove, finely chopped

1 sprig of fresh thyme

3 tablespoons crème fraîche or sour cream

salt and freshly ground black pepper

chopped fresh flat-leaf parsley, to garnish

Serves 4

Begin by scalding the tomatoes. Pour boiling water over the ripe tomatoes in a heatproof bowl. Set aside for 1 minute, then drain and carefully peel off the skin using a sharp knife.

Heat the oil in a small, heavy-bottomed frying pan/skillet set over a low heat. Add the shallot, garlic and thyme leaves and fry gently, stirring, for 2 minutes. Add the whole peeled tomatoes and fry for 5 minutes, stirring gently from time to time.

Add the crème fraîche or sour cream and season with salt and pepper. Increase the heat and bring to the boil. Cook for a further 5 minutes.

Garnish with parsley and serve at once.

Devilled tomatoes

As their name suggests, these tomatoes have a devilish peppery kick. Serve for breakfast or bunch alone or with bacon and eggs, or as an accompaniment for a roast ham.

2 tablespoons Dijon mustard

2 tablespoons creamed horseradish sauce

1 garlic clove, peeled and crushed

1 teaspoon white sugar

1 teaspoon white wine vinegar

a dash of Worcestershire sauce

a pinch of cayenne pepper

4 vine tomatoes

15 g/$\frac{1}{4}$ cup fresh breadcrumbs

a baking sheet, greased

Serves 2–4

Preheat the oven to 200°C (400°F) Gas 6.

Mix together the mustard, horseradish sauce, garlic, sugar, vinegar, Worcestershire sauce and cayenne pepper into a paste.

Slice the tomatoes in half and place skin-side down on the prepared baking sheet. Top each tomato half with the mustard paste, spreading evenly to coat them. Sprinkle with the breadcrumbs and bake in the preheated oven for 20 minutes until golden-brown, finishing off under the grill/broiler if necessary.

Serve at once.

Tomato curry

Quick and easy to make, this tasty dish is ideal for a super-speedy mid-week meal after a busy day at the office. Serve with steamed basmati rice and an Indian flat bread such as chapati, paratha or roti.

1 tablespoon vegetable oil

6–8 curry leaves

1 teaspoon cumin seeds

½ teaspoon ground turmeric

400 g/14 oz. tomatoes, each tomato sliced into eight pieces

2 teaspoons ground coriander

½ teaspoon chilli powder

1 teaspoon dark brown sugar

salt and freshly ground black pepper

fresh coriander/cilantro, to garnish

Serves 4

Heat the oil in a large, heavy-bottomed frying pan/skillet. Add the curry leaves, cumin seeds and ground turmeric and fry, stirring, for a minute, until very fragrant.

Add the sliced tomatoes and stir to coat with the frying spices. Sprinkle over the ground coriander, chilli powder and sugar, and stir well. Season with salt and pepper.

Continue to cook, stirring often, for 3–5 minutes until the tomato slices are heated through but still retain their shape.

Garnish with fresh coriander/cilantro and serve at once.

Tarka tomato dal

Tomatoes are excellent paired with earthy pulses; they have an enlivening effect on them. This satisfying dish is a classic example of Indian comfort food.

200 g/1 cup split red lentils

300 g/10 oz. tomatoes

1 tablespoon oil

1 onion, peeled and chopped

3 garlic cloves, peeled and chopped

a 5-cm/2-in. piece of fresh ginger, peeled and chopped

a handful of curry leaves

1 tablespoon tomato purée/paste

½ teaspoon ground turmeric

½ teaspoon chilli powder

a pinch of salt

1 teaspoon brown sugar

Tarka (hot, flavoured oil)

1 tablespoon ghee or oil

1 garlic clove, peeled and chopped

2 teaspoons cumin seeds

Serves 4

Rinse the lentils under cold, running water, then transfer to a large mixing bowl. Cover with cold water and set aside to soak for 30 minutes.

Scald the tomatoes following the instructions on page 17. Roughly chop, reserving the juices.

Heat the oil in a heavy-bottomed saucepan or pot set over a medium heat. Fry the onion, garlic and ginger for 2–3 minutes, stirring often, until softened and fragrant. Stir in the chopped tomatoes, curry leaves, tomato purée/paste, turmeric and chilli powder.

Drain the lentils and add to the pan with 300 ml/1¼ cups of water. Season with salt and stir in the sugar.

Bring to the boil, then cover partly, reduce the heat and simmer for 20–30 minutes, stirring often, until the lentils are soft and the water has been absorbed.

When the lentils are cooked, prepare the tarka. Heat the ghee in a small frying pan/skillet set over a medium heat. Add the garlic and fry until golden-brown. Add the cumin seeds and fry until fragrant. Pour the sizzling tarka over the dal and serve.

Festivals

Such is the affection in which tomatoes are held that people hold festivals and events celebrating them all over the world. Maybe it's their inherently cheerful, bright red colour or their soft, sweet juiciness that makes them a very accessible, easy-to-like food, which lends to them being celebrated. Usually, these events take place in areas associated with the growing of tomatoes and, naturally, they tend to take place during the summer months, when tomatoes are traditionally in season and tomato producers enjoy a glut of this wonderful fruit. In the USA, for example, the state of California is a major producer of tomatoes for the North American market. The summer months in the 'Sunshine State', therefore, see

a range of tomato-centric events, ranging from celebrations of heritage varieties, featuring chefs competing to create the best tomato-based menus, to salsa festivals.

One of the best-known of America's tomato festivals was the Tomatofest at Carmel, a tomato harvest festival complete with hundreds of heirloom tomato varieties, tomato cookery classes and tastings for tomato salsas. Established by Gary Ibsen (see page 117) in 1990 and running until 2008, it was a celebration of all 600 heirloom tomato varieties he grows, which raised money for children's charities. The glorious diversity of tomato varieties available is often a cause for celebration, allowing for taste comparisons and competitions. The Seed Savers Exchange in America, for example, dedicated to preserving and promoting heirloom vegetables through its seed bank, holds tomato-tasting workshops with sampling of heritage varieties such as Dester or Lemon Drop in order to find the tastiest among them and herald celebration of them.

Many communities around the world celebrate tomato varieties local to them. In southern Italy, the San Marzano tomato is the focus for many *sagre*, the local, grass-roots festivals often centred on a specific food type. The tomatoes produced in San Marzano are considered by many to be the best. They are thinner and more pointed than salad tomatoes, the flesh is much tougher, with fewer seeds and the taste is strong and sweet. In New Orleans, the locally grown Creole tomato, a summertime treat found growing on patios and in backyards, is at the heart of a festival in the city's historic French Quarter. The tradition of auctioning off the first box of ripe Creole tomatoes to local chefs at the French Market has become a feature of this Creole Tomato Festival.

One of the most famous tomato festivals, however, is La Tomatina, an exuberant and noticeably messy event which takes place on the last Wednesday of August each year, during the hot, sunny summer in Buñol, Valencia, in Spain. Within Europe, Spain is a major producer of tomatoes, supplying 35 per cent of Europe's tomato production and around 5.5 per cent of the world production. And, within Spain, Valencia is one of the country's best-known tomato growing regions. Rather than focusing on the eating of tomatoes, however, La Tomatina is, in fact, a massive tomato fight, which sees juicy, ripe tomatoes hurled through the air by thousands of energetic participants – billed by its organisers as 'the world's biggest food fight'.

The origins of La Tomatina are said to date back to the 1940s and there are various theories as to how it began. One theory is that young men from the town had a fight in the town square and resorted to hurling fruit and vegetables from a vegetable stall, creating what became an annual event. Another version is that it began as a protest against local politicians, with citizens resorting to the handiest – and messiest – of natural missiles, abundantly to hand. A third theory attributes La Tomatina's roots to an accidental spillage by a lorry laden with fresh tomatoes… The event was banned during the 1950s, but such was the depth of local feeling against the ban – with a mock 'tomato' funeral held in 1957 to protest against the ban – that it was allowed to be revived. Over the intervening decades, the event has grown enormously and is now a major tourist attraction, bringing in thousands of visitors from around the world each year. Such is the interest that the local authorities have now restricted access, making it a ticket-only event and limiting the number of participants to 20,000, rather than the 40–50,000 tomato-throwers and participants previously in attendance.

Truckloads laden with around 125 tonnes of ripe tomatoes are driven into Buñol to provide the 'ammunition' for the battle. During the hour-long fight, thousands of crushed tomatoes are hurled through the air, with participating revellers advised to wear swimwear, goggles and plastic gloves. Rules are in place, among them the squashing of tomatoes before hurling them in order to make these missiles softer. Following the event, the streets of Buñol run red with tomato pulp and juice, with contestants similarly covered from head to foot. Naturally, in these days of social media, sites are awash with striking images from the event of contestants floundering in a sea of squashed tomatoes. Its appeal is such that La Tomatina has inspired similar events all around the world, in countries including China, the UK and the USA. The original tomato fight in Spain's Buñol, however, retains its loyal following.

Puy lentils in sage and tomato sauce

Tomatoes and lentils are a classic combination. Serve this hearty dish as a side with robust-flavoured meat dishes such as roast pork belly with garlic, beef stews or Italian *salsicce* (sausages), or a main with crusty bread.

200 g/1 cup Puy/green
   lentils
1 tablespoon olive oil
½ onion, peeled and
   chopped
½ carrot, peeled and
   finely sliced
1 celery stick, finely
   chopped
4 fresh sage leaves,
   shredded
a glug of red wine
400 g/14½ oz. canned
   peeled plum tomatoes
salt and freshly ground
   black pepper
cooked pork or
   vegetarian sausages
   (optional)

*Serves 4 as a side
dish and 2 as a main*

Rinse the lentils under cold, running water. Put them in a saucepan or pot, cover with cold water and bring to the boil over a medium heat. Reduce heat and simmer for 10–15 minutes, until tender; drain.

Meanwhile, heat the oil in a heavy-bottomed saucepan or pot set over a medium heat. Add the onion, carrot and celery and cook for 2–3 minutes, until softened. Sprinkle over the sage and pour in the wine. Cook briskly for 1 minute before adding the canned tomatoes. Season with salt and pepper and bring to the boil. Reduce the heat and simmer for 15 minutes, stirring now and then to break up the tomatoes.

Mix the drained lentils into the tomato sauce and warm through. Add the cooked sausages if desired and serve at once.

Spinach tomato soufflé

A light-textured soufflé, presented straight from the oven, makes an elegant meal. Serve this with a crisp green side salad.

500 g/1 lb. fresh spinach

300 g/10 oz. ripe tomatoes

½ tablespoon olive oil

1 small onion, peeled and finely chopped

1 bay leaf

1 tablespoon tomato purée/paste

50 g/3 tablespoons butter

50 g/5 tablespoons flour

200 ml/¾ cup warm whole milk

salt and freshly ground black pepper

freshly grated nutmeg

5 eggs, separated, plus 1 egg white

2 litre/1 quart soufflé dish, greased

Serves 6

Preheat the oven to 200°C (400°F) Gas 6.

Rinse the spinach under cold, running water. Put it in a saucepan or pot, cover with boiling water and set over a medium heat. Cook for 2–3 minutes until wilted; drain, cool, squeeze dry and roughly chop.

Next, scald the tomatoes. Pour boiling water over the ripe tomatoes in a heatproof bowl. Set aside for 1 minute, then drain and carefully peel off the skin using a sharp knife. Roughly chop, reserving any juices, and set aside.

Heat the oil in a frying pan/skillet set over a medium heat. Add the onion and bay leaf and fry for 2 minutes, until softened. Add the chopped tomatoes and their juices, cover and cook for 5 minutes. Uncover, mix with a wooden spoon to help the tomatoes break down, stir in the tomato purée/paste and cook uncovered for 5 minutes to form a thick sauce. Remove and discard the bay leaf.

In a separate heavy-bottomed saucepan or pot set over a medium heat, melt the butter. Mix in the flour, stirring well. Gradually stir in the warm milk and cook, stirring continuously, until it thickens. Season with salt, pepper and nutmeg.

Remove the white sauce from heat. Mix in the tomato sauce, then the spinach. Check and adjust the seasoning if necessary. Beat in the egg yolks, one at a time, and set aside.

Whisk the egg whites until stiff peaks form. Stir a spoonful of the whisked egg white into the soufflé mixture to loosen it. Lightly and gently fold in the remaining whisked egg white. Pour into the prepared soufflé dish and bake in the preheated oven for 1 hour, until the soufflé is risen and golden brown. Serve at once.

Tomato Parmesan frittata

Serve this Italian tomato-flavoured omelette as a light lunch with a crisp green salad and crusty bread on the side.

450 g/1 lb. ripe tomatoes

1 tablespoon olive oil

1 onion, finely sliced

salt and freshly ground black pepper

5 eggs

2 tablespoons grated Parmesan cheese

2 tablespoons finely chopped fresh flat-leaf parsley

25 g/1½ tablespoons butter

a 20-cm/8-in. ovenproof frying pan/skillet

Serves 4

Halve the tomatoes, scoop out and discard the soft pulp and seeds, forming tomato shells. Thinly slice them and set aside.

Heat the oil in a heavy-bottomed frying pan/skillet set over a low heat. Add the onion and fry, stirring now and then, for 5 minutes until softened. Add the tomato slices and season with salt and pepper. Increase the heat and fry, stirring often, for 5 minutes until softened and pulpy. Set aside to cool.

Beat the eggs in a large mixing bowl and stir in the Parmesan cheese and parsley. Season with a little salt and pepper, bearing in mind the saltiness of the Parmesan. Mix in the cooled tomato mixture.

Heat the butter in the ovenproof frying pan/skillet over a medium–high heat, until frothy. Pour in the egg mixture, reduce the heat to low and cook gently for around 25 minutes.

Meanwhile, preheat the grill/broiler to a medium heat.

Place the frittata under the hot grill/broiler and cook for 3 minutes, until set and browned. Slice into quarters and serve hot or at room temperature.

Tomato herb roulade

This light and elegant concoction of tomatoes, eggs, ricotta and fresh herbs makes a wonderfully summery dish. Serve it for a light meal, accompanied by a crisp green side salad.

40 g/2½ tablespoons butter

1 bay leaf

40 g/⅓ cup plain/all-purpose flour

300 ml/1¼ cups whole milk

salt and freshly ground black pepper

3 tablespoons tomato purée/paste

3 eggs, separated

200 g/6½ oz. cherry tomatoes

300 g/10 oz. ricotta cheese

4 tablespoons each of finely chopped fresh flat-leaf parsley, basil leaves and chives

1 teaspoon finely grated lemon zest

2 tablespoons grated Parmesan cheese

a 23 x 32-cm/9 x 13-in. swiss/jelly roll baking pan, greased and lined with baking parchment

a baking sheet, greased

Serves 4

Preheat the oven to 200°C (400°F) Gas 6.

Melt the butter together with the bay leaf in a heavy-bottomed saucepan or pot set over a medium heat. Add the flour and cook, stirring, for 1 minute, to form a paste. Gradually stir in the milk and cook, stirring continuously, until thickened.

Transfer to a large mixing bowl, discard the bay leaf and season with salt and pepper. Stir in the tomato purée/paste, to form a tomato roux. Beat in the egg yolks, one by one.

Whisk the egg whites until stiff peaks form. Stir a spoonful of the whisked egg white into the tomato roux mixture to loosen it. Gently fold in the remaining whisked egg whites.

Gently spread the mixture evenly into the prepared baking pan. Bake in the preheated oven for 12–15 minutes until risen and set. Remove from the oven, cover with a clean kitchen cloth and set aside to cool.

Cut the tomatoes in half, scoop out the pulp and finely dice the tomato shells, leaving the skin on for texture.

Prepare the filling by mixing together the chopped tomatoes, ricotta cheese, herbs and lemon zest, seasoning with pepper.

Uncover the cooled roulade and spread evenly with the tomato mixture. Roll up the roulade from the short side, forming a long roll. Transfer to the prepared baking sheet.

Sprinkle the roulade with the grated Parmesan and bake in the preheated oven for 20 minutes.

Serve in slices warm from the oven.

Provençal stuffed tomatoes

A satisfying classic French tomato dish, flavoured simply with fresh herbs, shallot and garlic. Serve as a light lunch or as a side to baked chicken.

4 large, firm-fleshed tomatoes, such as Coeur de Boeuf, Brandywine or other beefsteak tomato (each about 250 g/8 oz.)

salt and freshly ground black pepper

4 tablespoons olive oil

1 shallot, peeled and finely chopped

1 garlic clove, peeled and finely chopped

150 g/2¼ cups fresh breadcrumbs

1 teaspoon fresh thyme leaves

1 tablespoon chopped fresh chives

2 tablespoons chopped fresh flat-leaf parsley

grated zest of 1 lemon

2 tablespoons grated Parmesan cheese

Serves 4

Preheat the oven to 200°C (400°F) Gas 6.

Cutting across, slice a 'cap' off the top of each tomato, so as to reveal the seedy pulp inside. Using a small, sharp knife, carefully loosen the pulp from the tomato sides, then scrape out with a spoon, making four hollow tomato shells. Sprinkle inside the tomato shells with a little salt to draw out the juices, then turn upside down and set aside.

Heat the oil in a heavy-bottomed frying pan/skillet set over a low heat. Add the shallot and garlic and fry gently, stirring often, until softened, without allowing it to brown. Add the breadcrumbs, mix well and fry for 1–2 minutes. Remove the pan from the heat and stir in the thyme, chives, parsley and lemon zest. Season with salt and pepper.

Arrange the tomato shells in the prepared baking dish and fill them with the breadcrumb mixture. Top with a the grated Parmesan cheese.

Bake in the preheated oven for 30 minutes until the Parmesan cheese is golden-brown. Serve hot or at room temperature.

Menemen

A classic Turkish dish, this colourful version of scrambled eggs is great for a flavourful breakfast or brunch. Serve menemen with rustic bread, a crisp baguette or toast.

200 g/½ lb. tomatoes

6 eggs

½ teaspoon Turkish pepper flakes, such as Aleppo pepper

1 teaspoon fresh thyme leaves

salt and freshly ground black pepper

7 g/½ tablespoon butter

1 tablespoon olive oil

2 spring onions/scallions, chopped

½ green (bell) pepper, chopped

2 teaspoons tomato purée/paste

2 tablespoons chopped fresh flat-leaf parsley

Serves 4

Begin by scalding the tomatoes. Pour boiling water over the ripe tomatoes in a heatproof bowl. Set aside for 1 minute, then drain and carefully peel off the skin using a sharp knife. Roughly chop, reserving any juices, and set aside.

Beat the eggs in a large mixing bowl and season with the Turkish pepper flakes, thyme, salt and pepper.

Heat the butter and oil in a large, heavy-bottomed frying pan/skillet set over a low heat. Add the spring onions/scallions and (bell) pepper and fry gently, stirring, for 2 minutes. Add the chopped tomatoes and cook, stirring often, for 8–10 minutes, until the tomatoes have softened and form a thick paste. Add the tomato purée/paste, mixing in well.

Pour in the beaten, seasoned eggs and gently stir. Cook, stirring gently now and then, until the eggs are to your taste.

Garnish with parsley and serve at once.

rice and pasta dishes

Mexican red rice

Tomatoes give a delicate sweetness to the rice here, with a touch of heat from the chilli/chile. Serve as a tasty side dish with grilled chicken or steak and a tomato salsa.

200 g/½ lb. tomatoes

1 tablespoon vegetable oil

½ onion, peeled and finely chopped

1 garlic clove, peeled and sliced

1 red chilli/chile, chopped

200 g/1 cup long-grain rice, rinsed

250 ml/1 cup chicken or vegetable stock

salt, to taste

50 g/½ cup frozen peas (optional)

Serves 4

Begin by scalding the tomatoes. Pour boiling water over the ripe tomatoes in a heatproof bowl. Set aside for 1 minute, then drain and carefully peel off the skin using a sharp knife. Roughly chop, reserving any juices, and set aside.

Heat the oil in a heavy-bottomed saucepan or pot set over a medium heat. Add the onion and garlic and fry until softened. Add the chilli/chile and fry for another minute, then add the chopped tomatoes with their juices. Increase the heat, stir well, and cook until the tomatoes have broken down and form a thick paste.

Mix in the rice and pour over the stock. Season with salt, bring the mixture to the boil and add the frozen peas, if using. Cover, reduce the heat and cook for 10–15 minutes until the stock has been absorbed and the rice is cooked through.

Tomato risotto

There is something inherently satisfying about a well-made risotto, a perfect meal at the end of a long day. The soft, cooked rice is given a lovely lift by stirring in the diced fresh tomato and a little lemon zest.

1 litre/4¼ cups chicken or vegetable stock

50 g/3 tablespoons butter

1 tablespoon olive oil

1 shallot, peeled and finely chopped

1 celery stick, finely chopped

1 anchovy fillet in oil (about 10 g/⅓ oz.)

300 g/1½ cups risotto rice

100 ml/scant ½ cup tomato passata/ strained tomatoes (see page 149)

salt and freshly ground black pepper

100 g/3½ oz. ripe tomatoes, scalded (see page 17), skinned and finely diced

grated zest of 1 lemon

1 tablespoon chopped fresh flat-leaf parsley

grated Parmesan cheese, to serve

Serves 4

Bring the stock to a simmer in a saucepan or pot set over a low–medium heat.

Heat 25 g/1½ tablespoons of the butter and al the oil in a large, heavy-bottomed saucepan or pot set over a medium heat. Once the mixture is frothing, add the shallot and celery. Fry, stirring, for 2 minutes, until softened. Add the anchovy and fry, stirring, until it melts into the mixture.

Add the rice to the pan and stir, coating with the mixture. Pour in 150 ml/⅔ cup of the simmering stock and all the tomato passata/strained tomatoes. Season with salt and pepper and cook, stirring constantly, until the liquid has been largely absorbed by the rice. Add in another 150 ml/⅔ cup of simmering stock and repeat until until all the stock has been used and the rice is cooked through.

Stir through the remaining butter, then gently fold in the tomatoes, lemon zest and parsley.

Serve at once with grated Parmesan cheese.

Jollof rice

An African classic, this tasty one-pot combination of rice, tomatoes and chicken is a hearty example of comfort food.

450 g/1 lb. tomatoes

2 tablespoons vegetable oil

4 chicken breast fillets, chopped

1 onion, peeled and chopped

1 garlic clove, peeled and chopped

1/2 red (bell) pepper, chopped

300 g/1 1/2 cups long-grain rice, rinsed

1 carrot, peeled and sliced

50 g/1 cup green beans, topped, tailed and sliced

2 tablespoons tomato purée/paste

1 Scotch bonnet or habanero chilli/chile, finely chopped

350 ml/1 1/3 cup chicken or vegetable stock

a pinch of salt

chopped fresh flat-leaf parsley, to garnish

Serves 6

Begin by scalding the tomatoes. Pour boiling water over the ripe tomatoes in a heatproof bowl. Set aside for 1 minute, then drain and carefully peel off the skin using a sharp knife. Roughly chop, reserving any juices, and set aside.

Heat 1 tablespoon of the oil in a heavy-bottomed casserole dish set over a medium heat. Add the chicken and fry, stirring, for a few minutes until lightly browned on all sides; season with a little salt and remove with a slotted spoon.

Put the remaining oil in the casserole dish. Add the onion, garlic and (bell) pepper and fry, stirring, for 2–3 minutes, until softened. Add the chopped tomatoes with their juices, cover, bring to the boil and cook for 5 minutes, stirring now and then.

Add the fried chicken, rice, carrot and green beans and mix in the tomato purée/paste. Add the Scotch bonnet or habanero chilli/ chile, pour in the stock and season with salt. Bring to the boil, cover, reduce the heat and cook for 25–30 minutes until the liquid has been absorbed and the rice is tender.

Garnish with parsley and serve at once.

Meet the growers

It is all too easy to take the convenient abundance of tomatoes we are offered in greengrocers, farmers' markets and supermarkets for granted. To do so, however, is to forget the sheer hard labour and horticultural knowledge which goes into cultivating tomatoes. Growing tomatoes for yourself brings home quite how much care and attention is required. This is especially so when it comes to heritage tomato varieties, which, by their nature, are often less robust and offer smaller crop yields. Fortunately, the rich range of tomato varieties we enjoy is preserved by committed growers around the world, four of whom we have profiled here in tribute to their hard work. Growing tomatoes in the Italy, the UK, Spain and the USA, each one of these growers champions heritage and speciality tomatoes. All of them are doing invaluable work to maintain the wonderful diversity of the tomato plant, so that we can enjoy the fruits of their labours.

DANICOOP, CAMPANIA, ITALY

When it comes to Italian tomatoes, the jewel in the crown is the famous San Marzano tomato. Granted Denominazione di Origine Protetta (DOP) status, meaning 'Protected Designation of Origin', the authentic San Marzano tomato is grown in specific areas in southern Italy, close to Naples, and here alone. This long-shaped, thin-skinned tomato, bright red in colour, is noted for its particular bitter-sweet flavour, low acidity and firm flesh. Its thick flesh and comparative lack of seeds means that it lends itself well to all forms of preserving, with canned San Marzano tomatoes famed worldwide.

Danicoop, headed by Paolo Ruggero, a champion of the 'pomodoro San Marzano DOP', is an agricultural cooperative of local farmers who grow San Marzano tomatoes in Nocerino Sarnese, an area listed by the DOP, which is in the Sarno Valley, near Naples. Thanks to nearby Vesuvius and the Sarno river, the soil here is rich and fertile, playing an integral part in creating the tomato's characteristic taste. Danicoop conscientiously maintain the traditional cultivation and processing methods, growing the tomatoes outdoors, using manual spring water irrigation and hand-picking the tomatoes only when they are fully ripe in the period between July and September; these are then canned using a water bath (*bagnomaria*) system. Provenance, agricultural history and intense flavour come together here in an appetizing and satisfying fashion.

NUTBOURNE NURSERY, WEST SUSSEX, UK

Founded in 1979, this small nursery business, run by husband-and-wife-team Gary and Jenny Griffiths, champions the British-grown speciality tomato. Gary, the son of a greengrocer, has a long experience of growing tomatoes in greenhouses and continues to be fascinated by both tomatoes and the challenges of growing them. Here at

Nutbourne he grows around 27 varieties of tomato, all chosen for their flavour, working within their natural season from February to October, rather than all year round.

Growing the different varieties within one large greenhouse offers challenges, as each have different specific needs. As such, much patient work watering, feeding, pruning side-shoots, nipping back trusses, moving the plants so that they receive the light they need goes into the tomatoes that Nutbourne produces. These perfectly ripe tomatoes, from pineapple Marmande to Tiger varieties, are then packed up and delivered by Gary himself to the restaurants and farm shops that he supplies. The advantage of growing and supplying British tomatoes in the way that he does is that his tomatoes are delivered freshly picked that day, with no need for cold storage, protective packaging or a long supply chain. The tasty results of his labours are much appreciated by the chefs at the restaurants Nutbourne supplies, a fact that gives Gary considerable satisfaction.

TOMATOFEST, USA

An epiphany during the 1980s, when eating a freshly picked, ripe heirloom tomato grown by a Portuguese farmer down the road, led Gary Ibsen to a life spent growing and promoting heirloom tomatoes. So struck was he by its flavour and sweetness, in contrast to the insipid tomatoes on offer in supermarkets, that he set off to discover more about them, finding and collecting tomato seeds from keen gardeners. By 'heirloom', Gary means old-fashioned tomatoes, treasured for their flavour, passed down for generations within families in America and around the world. Gary, known simply as 'The Tomato Man', and his wife Dagmar founded Tomatofest, growing heirloom tomatoes outdoors in the warm Californian sunshine on certified organic soil, rich

in nutrients, with the plants watered with their own organic compost 'tea' to feed them. The tomatoes are harvested when they have fully ripened on the vine and the seeds gathered from their own tomatoes are sold in packets.

Today, Gary grows over 600 tomato varieties, from vintage Martina, Brandywine amd Black Cherry heirloom tomatoes to wonderfully named exclusive tomatoes such as Clint Eastwood's Rowdy Red.

HUESCA GROWERS, SPAIN

As one would expect from the country oft credited with introducing tomatoes to Europe, Spain has a long and venerable history of cultivating tomatoes. Indeed, nowadays it is one of the major European producers of tomatoes, both fresh and processed. Within Spain itself, delicate pink tomatoes (*tomate rosado*) have been grown and enjoyed for centuries, and are a hallmark of many traditional Andalusian dishes.

An increased awareness of the importance of preserving Spain's rich food heritage has seen a move to protect and promote the pink tomato from Barbastro in Huesca. Large pink-hued tomatoes, weighing around 500 g/18 oz. each, with a fine skin, the flesh has very few seeds and has a notably sweet flavour and fragrance. These tomatoes are low in acidity, making them an excellent salad tomato. Traditionally, pink tomatoes in the Huesca province have always been grown on a small scale by local gardeners, making the most of the rich soil and sunshine, with the crops sold in the region's food markets. The Barbastro pink tomato is too fragile for exporting over long distances, so has remained a local speciality enjoyed near where it is grown. Championing traditional methods of cultivation, the Asociacion de Hortelanos del Alto Aragon comprises local tomato growers committed to retaining this special tomato.

Tomato almond pilaff

Delicately flavoured with fragrant spices, this pretty rice dish is an excellent accompaniment to dishes such as marinated roast lamb or baked fish.

25 g/1½ tablespoons butter

1 shallot, peeled and finely chopped

1 cinnamon stick

2 cardamom pods

200 g/1 cup basmati rice, rinsed

1 tablespoon tomato purée/paste

a pinch of salt

225 g/½ lb. tomatoes

25 g/3 tablespoons flaked/slivered almonds, dry-fried until golden

chopped fresh coriander/cilantro, to garnish

Serves 4

Heat the butter in a heavy-bottomed saucepan or pot set over a medium heat. Add the shallot, cinnamon stick and cardamom pods and fry gently, stirring now and then, for 2 minutes, until the shallot softens.

Mix in the basmati rice, coating well with the butter, then the tomato purée/paste. Pour over 300 ml/1¼ cups of water and season with salt. Bring the mixture to the boil, reduce the heat, cover and simmer for 10–15 minutes, until the water has all been absorbed and the rice is tender.

Meanwhile, scald the tomatoes. Pour boiling water over the tomatoes in a small pan or pot set over a medium heat. Heat for 1 minute, then remove from the water and carefully peel off the skin using a sharp knife. Halve the tomatoes, scoop out the soft pulp and finely dice the tomato shells.

When the rice is cooked, transfer to a serving dish. Fold in the diced tomatoes, sprinkle with the flaked/slivered almonds and coriander/cilantro, and serve at once.

Tomato macaroni cheese

Comfort eating is on offer here, with this satisfying version of the much-loved classic, mac 'n' cheese. Serve with a green side salad for a hearty lunch or supper.

1/2 tablespoon olive oil

1 shallot or 1/2 onion, finely chopped

1 bay leaf

200 g/6 1/2 oz. canned chopped tomatoes

225 g/8 oz. macaroni or penne dried pasta

25 g/1 1/2 tablespoons butter

25 g/2 1/2 tablespoons flour

400 ml/1 2/3 cups whole milk

salt and freshly ground black pepper

freshly grated nutmeg

75 g/1 cup grated Cheddar cheese

8 cherry tomatoes, halved

10 g/3 tablespoons fresh breadcrumbs

Serves 4

Heat the oil in a frying pan/skillet set over a medium heat. Add the shallot and bay leaf and fry, stirring, for 2 minutes, until the shallot has softened. Add the canned tomatoes, season with salt and pepper and fry, stirring now and then, for 2–3 minutes. Remove and discard the bay leaf, then blend until smooth.

Cook the macaroni pasta in salted, boiling water until tender, then drain.

Preheat the grill/broiler to a medium heat.

Make the cheese sauce by melting the butter in a heavy-bottomed saucepan or pot set over a medium heat. Stir in the flour and cook, stirring continuously, for 1 minute. Gradually pour in the milk, stirring well as you do. Season well with salt, pepper and nutmeg. Bring to the boil, stirring all the time, reduce the heat and simmer until the sauce thickens. Stir in 25 g/1/3 cup of the Cheddar cheese until melted, then mix in the tomato sauce.

Place the cooked macaroni in a shallow, heatproof dish. Pour over the tomato–cheese sauce, mix well, then stir in the cherry tomatoes. Top with the remaining Cheddar cheese and the breadcrumbs, sprinkling evenly.

Grill/broil for around 10 minutes, until golden-brown and bubbling hot. Serve at once.

Crab, tomato and basil linguine

Very quick to cook, this simple combination makes a stylish pasta dish.
Serve as a main course accompanied by a crisp-textured side salad.

250 g/½ lb. ripe tomatoes

400 g/14 oz. linguine

4 tablespoons olive oil

2 garlic cloves, peeled and finely chopped

300 g/10 oz. fresh crab meat (white and brown)

1 red chilli/chile, finely chopped

50 ml/1¾ oz. dry white wine

freshly ground black pepper

a handful of fresh basil leaves, shredded

Serves 4

Begin by scalding the tomatoes. Pour boiling water over the ripe tomatoes in a heatproof bowl. Set aside for 1 minute, then drain and carefully peel off the skin using a sharp knife. Halve the tomatoes, scoop out the soft pulp and finely dice the tomato.

Bring a large saucepan or pot of salted water to the boil over a high heat. Add the linguine and cook for 8–10 minutes, until *al dente*. Drain and keep warm.

Meanwhile, heat the oil in a frying pan/skillet set over a medium heat. Add the garlic and fry briefly until fragrant. Then add the crab meat, chilli/chile and wine. Season with pepper and cook, stirring, for 2–3 minutes until the wine has cooked down to form a sauce. Stir in the diced tomato.

Toss together the drained linguine, sauce and basil, ensuring the pasta is well coated in sauce. Serve at once.

Aubergine lasagne

A great vegetarian take on a much-loved classic pasta dish, this combines the satisfying texture of aubergines/eggplant with a fresh tomato and creamy white sauce. This is delicious home-cooked food with an Italian touch.

1 kg/1¼ lbs. ripe tomatoes

5 tablespoons olive oil

1 onion, peeled and chopped

1 garlic clove, peeled and chopped

salt and freshly ground black pepper

a handful of fresh basil leaves

2 aubergines/eggplant, finely diced

25 g/2 tablespoons butter

25 g/3½ tablespoons flour

300 ml/1¼ cups milk

freshly grated nutmeg

about 12 cooked lasagne sheets

25 g/⅓ cup freshly grated Parmesan cheese

Serves 4

Begin by scalding and skinning the tomatoes following the instructions on page 17. Roughly chop, reserving any juices, and set aside.

Heat 1 tablespoon of the oil in a large, heavy-bottomed frying pan/skillet over a low heat. Fry the onion and garlic until softened. Add the chopped tomatoes with their juices. Season with salt and pepper.

Increase the heat, cover and bring the mixture to the boil. Uncover and cook for a further 5 minutes, stirring often, until reduced and thickened. Stir in the basil.

Heat 2 tablespoons of the oil in a separate large, heavy-bottomed frying pan/skillet set over a medium heat. Add half of the diced aubergine/eggplant and fry, stirring often, until softened and lightly browned, then set aside. Repeat the process with the remaining oil and aubergine/eggplant. Mix the fried aubergine/eggplant into the tomato sauce.

Preheat the oven to 200°C (400°F) Gas 6.

Make a white sauce by melting the butter in a heavy-bottomed saucepan or pot set over a low–medium heat. Stir in the flour and cook, stirring, for 1–2 minutes. Gradually pour in the milk, stirring continuously to combine. Bring the mixture to the boil and simmer until thickened. Season with salt, pepper and nutmeg.

Arrange a layer of lasagne sheets in the bottom of an ovenproof dish. Put an even layer of the aubergine/eggplant mixture over the top, then sprinkle over a little grated Parmesan cheese. Repeat the process, finishing with a layer of lasagne sheets. Spread the white sauce evenly over the top, then sprinkle over the remaining Parmesan.

Bake for 40–50 minutes in the preheated oven until golden-brown. Remove from the oven and serve at once.

Polenta puttanesca

A feisty, spicy Italian tomato sauce contrasts nicely with the comforting blandness of grilled polenta in this hearty dish.

200 g/1⅓ cups instant polenta

2 tablespoons olive oil

1 garlic clove, peeled and chopped

6 anchovy fillets in oil, chopped

800 g/1¾ lbs. canned peeled cherry tomatoes

2 small dried chillies/chiles, finely chopped

2 teaspoons capers, rinsed

2 generous pinches of dried oregano

freshly ground black pepper

chopped fresh flat-leaf parsley, to garnish

a 23-cm/9-in. square baking pan, greased

Serves 4

First, prepare the polenta. Put the polenta and 800 ml/3⅓ cups of cold water in a large saucepan or pot and season well with salt. Set over a medium–high heat and bring to the boil, stirring continuously. Reduce the heat and simmer, stirring often, until the polenta thickens and begins to come away from the sides of the pan. Transfer to the prepared baking pan, patting smooth with the back of a spoon and set aside to cool.

While the polenta is cooling, prepare the puttanesca sauce. Heat the olive oil in large frying pan/skillet set over a medium heat. Add the garlic and fry until fragrant. Then add the anchovy fillets and fry until they melt in the pan. Mix in the cherry tomatoes, dried chillies/chiles, capers and oregano and season with pepper. Cook, stirring often, for 15–20 minutes, until the sauce has reduced and thickened.

Preheat the oven to 110°C (225°F) Gas ¼.

Cut the cooled, set polenta into 8 even-sized squares.

Preheat an oiled, ridged stovetop grill pan until very hot, then cook the polenta in batches until marked by the griddle on each side, keeping each square warm in the preheated oven.

Gently heat through the puttanesca sauce over a low heat, then spoon over the grilled polenta squares and sprinkle over the parsley, to serve.

breads and pastry

Summer tomato tart

Gloriously simple to make, this Mediterranean-flavoured tart tastes as good as it looks. If available, use different coloured tomatoes for the topping for extra visual appeal. Serve for a light meal accompanied by a crisp green side salad.

300 g/10 oz. puff pastry dough

400 g/1 lb. ripe tomatoes

2 tablespoons black olive tapenade

salt and freshly ground black pepper

a handful of fresh basil leaves, to garnish

a baking sheet, greased

Serves 6

On a lightly floured surface, thinly roll out the puff pastry to form a circle about 27 cm/11 in. in diameter. Chill the pastry circle in the fridge for 30 minutes.

Preheat the oven to 200°C (400°F) Gas 6.

Cut the tomatoes into 0.5-cm/^{3}/$_{16}$-in. thick slices.

Place the chilled pastry circle on the prepared baking sheet. Spread the olive tapenade evenly over the pastry, leaving a 2-cm/^{3}/$_4$-in. rim around the edge. Arrange the tomato slices in spiraling rings over the tapenade, overlapping them slightly. Season with a little salt and pepper, bearing in mind the saltiness of the tapenade.

Bake in the preheated oven for 40 minutes, then reduce the oven temperature to 150°C (300°F) Gas 2 and bake for a further 1 hour, until the pastry is crisp and golden-brown and the tomatoes are cooked through.

Serve either warm from the oven or at room temperature, garnished with basil leaves.

Tomato fennel buns

Sun-dried tomato purée/paste and fennel seeds add a rich and distinctive flavour to these luxurious rolled buns. Serve warm from the oven for breakfast or brunch.

300 g/2⅓ cups plain/
 all-purpose white flour

½ teaspoon salt

½ teaspoon fast-action
 dried yeast

1 teaspoon caster/
 granulated sugar

75 g/5 tablespoons
 butter, diced

3 tablespoons warm
 whole milk

2 eggs, beaten

3 tablespoons sun-dried
 tomato purée/paste

8 sun-blush tomatoes in
 oil, chopped

1 teaspoon fennel seeds

1 egg yolk, beaten, for
 glazing

a large mixing bowl, oiled

a 20-cm/8-in. square
 baking pan, greased
 and lined with baking
 parchment

Makes 12

Sift the flour into a large mixing bowl. Stir through the salt, yeast and sugar. Using your fingertips, rub the butter into the flour mixture until it resembles breadcrumbs. Pour in the milk and stir together quickly. Stir in the beaten eggs and mix together well to form a soft, sticky dough. Turn out onto a lightly floured surface and knead until smooth and elastic. Transfer to an oiled mixing bowl, cover with a clean damp kitchen cloth and set aside in a warm place to rise for 1 hour.

Break down the risen dough and pat out into a large rectangle, measuring about 30 x 23 cm/12 x 9 in. Spread the dough with a thin layer of the sun-dried tomato purée/paste and sprinkle evenly with sun-blush tomatoes and fennel seeds. Roll the dough up lengthways, like a Swiss roll or roulade. Cut into 12 even slices. Place the slices, cut side-up, in the prepared baking pan. Cover with a clean kitchen cloth and set aside for 30 minutes.

Preheat the oven to 200°C (400°F) Gas 6.

Brush the buns with the beaten egg yolk, then bake in the preheated oven for 20–25 minutes until golden-brown.

Serve warm from the oven or at room temperature.

Sun-dried tomato and rosemary corn bread

This quick, easy and tasty cornbread goes well with soup, such as the Tomato and roast squash soup on page 37, and brunch dishes such as the Tunisian baked eggs in tomato sauce on page 87.

130 g/1 cup plain/
  all-purpose flour

130 g/1 cup fine cornmeal

2 tablespoons white
  sugar

2 teaspoons baking
  powder

½ teaspoon salt

200 ml/¾ cup whole milk

2 eggs

50 g/3 tablespoons
  butter, melted

6 sun-dried tomatoes in
  oil, chopped into pieces

1 teaspoon finely chopped
  fresh rosemary leaves

*a 20-cm/8-in. square
  baking pan, greased
  and foil-lined*

*Makes 1 loaf and
serves 9*

Preheat the oven to 200°C (400°F) Gas 6.

Mix the flour, cornmeal, sugar, baking powder and salt together in a large mixing bowl.

In a separate bowl, whisk together the milk and eggs and stir in the melted butter.

Pour the milk mixture into the flour mixture and add in the sun-dried tomatoes and rosemary. Quickly fold together, taking care not to over-mix.

Transfer the mixture to the prepared baking pan and bake in the preheated oven for 30 minutes, until risen and golden-brown.

Serve at once, warm from the oven.

Triple tomato pizza

Homemade pizza is fun to make and to eat. This simple recipe offers
a classic combination of flavours: the fresh acidity of tomatoes, mild
mozzarella and salty anchovies.

500 g/4 cups strong
bread flour

1 teaspoon caster/
granulated sugar

1 teaspoon salt

1 teaspoon fast-action
dried yeast

300 ml/1¼ cups
lukewarm water

2 tablespoons olive oil

300 ml/1¼ cups
tomato passata/strained
tomatoes (see page 149)

8 sun-dried or sun-blush
tomatoes in oil,
chopped

8 cherry tomatoes, halved

2 balls fresh mozzarella,
chopped

8 anchovy fillets in oil
(each about 10 g/⅓ oz.)

fresh basil leaves, to
garnish

a large mixing bowl, oiled

*4 pizza stones or baking
sheets, lightly floured*

Makes 4

First, make the pizza dough. Mix together the flour, sugar, salt and
yeast. Gradually, pour in the lukewarm water and the oil, forming
a sticky dough. Turn out onto a lightly floured surface and knead
until smooth and elastic. Transfer to the prepared mixing bowl,
cover with a clean damp kitchen cloth and set aside in a warm
place to rise for 1 hour.

Preheat the oven to 240°C (475°F) Gas 9.

Break down the pizza dough and roll out on a lightly floured
surface to form 4 pizza bases.

Transfer each base to the prepared pizza stones or baking sheets.
You may have to bake one at a time, depending on the size of
your oven. Spread with tomato passata/strained tomatoes, leaving
a rim of plain dough around the edge. Top each pizza with the
sun-dried tomatoes, cherry tomatoes, mozzarella cheese and
anchovy fillets.

Bake the pizzas in the preheated oven for 10–15 minutes until the
mozzarella cheese has melted and the dough is golden. Sprinkle
with basil leaves and serve at once.

Saving our tomato heritage

Tomatoes exist in astonishing variety. There are thousands of different tomato varieties grown around the world, with different tomatoes ranging widely in colour, size, shape and flavour. A sense that the extraordinary genetic diversity was at risk of being lost, however, has seen the rise of organisations actively committing to sustaining it.

In the UK, for example, the Henry Doubleday Research Institute, now known as 'Garden Organic', was founded by Lawrence D Hills in 1954 to research and promote organic gardening. Among its many activities was the setting up of the Heritage Seed Programme in the 1970s, collecting tomato and other vegetable seed from small-scale growers, from which came the Heritage Seed Library, that aims to conserve and make available varietals that are not widely found across the country. The collection contains several family heirloom varieties of tomato which have not been sold commercially. The Library's work is supported by a network of Seed Guardians, who volunteer to grow and collect seed, which in turn, when enough seed is available, is shared among the members.

The USA, similarly, saw the Seed Savers Exchange established in 1975, a non-profit organisation dedicated to saving and sharing heirloom seeds, one of the largest seed banks of its kind in North America offering over 13,000 varieties of heirloom vegetable and fruit seeds. As with the Heritage Seed Library in the UK, the active commitment of its members is essential to its ability to maintain and grow seed stocks. It promotes 'participatory preservation' with its members growing and sharing seeds. The seeds are regenerated and stored in carefully controlled conditions, with cultural information on their histories recorded. Heirloom variety seeds are made available to members, with some of the collection, featuring nearly 90 tomato varieties, also sold to the public.

The influential Slow Food movement, founded in Italy in 1986 to protect food culture and biodiversity, protects and promotes a number of threatened tomato varieties around the world, championing rare tomatoes such as Argentina's platense tomato, with its irregular shape and ribbed appearance, bunch tomatoes from Busturia, in Spain's Basque country, and the pointed-tipped Vesuvio Piennolo cherry tomato from Campania, Italy.

While the term 'heritage' or 'heirloom' actually lacks legal or scientific definition, it is generally taken to mean older varieties. The definition of 'older' is, however, open to interpretation. The term might be used for varieties which are over 20 years old or applied to those which existed before 1939. The use of the term 'heritage' or 'heirloom' also has implications for how the tomato is grown. Large-scale industrial cultivation of tomatoes uses what are called F1 hybrids. These are the first generation of plants created by controlled cross pollination. Because of how they are created, seeds from F1 hybrids will not come true. The term heritage or heirloom tomatoes, in contrast, is often applied to tomatoes which are not used in large-scale cultivation and are open pollinated, with the seed they produce generally coming true when they are saved and planted. The term 'open pollinated' is often used on seed packets by heirloom or heritage seed companies committed to this process. Another definition of the term 'heritage' or 'heirloom' is that this is a tomato plant which at some point in its history owes its continued existence because it had its seed saved by amateurs.

Thankfully, the interest in saving and growing what are known as 'heritage' or 'heirloom' varieties is increasing. Influential chefs, such as Alice Waters of Chez Panisse in California, USA, or Raymond Blanc of Le Manoir aux Quat'

Saisons, UK, have done much to promote them. There is an increased awareness that many of these traditional varieties offer superior flavour as well as an intriguing appearance. One only has to think about the needs of a domestic gardener as opposed to those of a large-scale tomato grower, to see why these older varieties might taste better. Whereas a home-gardener will be growing flavourful tomatoes for his or her own consumption, able to harvest them by hand as they ripen, the economies of industrial-scale agriculture requires that the tomatoes ideally ripen together, so that they can be mechanically harvested at one time, and that the tomatoes will be able to withstand much handling as they are packed and transportation over long distances, hence the rise commercially of firm, thick-skinned tomatoes, rather than fragile, thin-skinned, more delicate tomatoes.

Many seed companies specializing in heirloom or heritage vegetables have been set up in recent years, offering interested home gardeners a chance to explore for themselves the fascinating world of wonderfully-named tomato varieties. From the Brandywine, named after Brandywine Creek in Pennsylvania to Chalk's Early Jewel, developed by James Chalk, Vintage Wine or Black Jewel tomatoes, there's pleanty to choose from. More and more, one finds heirloom tomatoes featuring on restaurant menus and offered for sale in farmers' markets and greengrocers, allowing those who are tomato eaters rather than tomato growers a chance to sample the tomato in all its multifarious abundance.

Blush tomato
and feta muffins

Who doesn't love a savoury muffin? These combine
the rich, crumbly textures of feta cheese with the
sweet, ripened flavour of sun-blush tomatoes. Enjoy
for breakfast, brunch, lunch or dinner alongside soups
or other hot meals.

75 g/5 tablespoons butter, melted

2 eggs

140 ml/²/₃ cup whole milk

300 g/2¹/₃ cups self-raising/rising
  flour

1 teaspoon baking powder

1 teaspoon salt

2–3 pinches of dried oregano

14 sun-blush tomatoes, chopped

100 g/3¹/₂ oz. feta cheese, diced

*2 x 6-hole muffin pans, lined with
  10 muffin cases*

Makes 10

Preheat the oven to 200°C (400°F) Gas 6.

Whisk together the melted butter, eggs and milk in a large mixing
bowl.

In a separate bowl, sift the flour and baking powder together, then
stir in the salt and oregano. Pour in the melted butter mixture and
quickly and lightly fold into the flour. Stir through the tomatoes
and feta. Divide the mixture evenly between the muffin cases.

Bake in the preheated oven for 20–25 minutes until risen and
golden-brown. Serve warm from the oven or at room temperature.

Cherry tomato and olive focaccia

Homemade focaccia, served warm from the oven, is a real treat. This colourful loaf, studded with red cherry tomatoes and black olives, makes a great mealtime centrepiece, accompanied by cheeses and charcuterie.

500 g/4 cups strong white/bread flour

1 teaspoon quick yeast

1 teaspoon salt

1 teaspoon sugar

300 ml/1¼ cups hand-hot water

5 tablespoons extra virgin olive oil

12 cherry tomatoes, halved

12 pitted black olives

a few sprigs of fresh

a pinch of sea salt flakes, to serve

a large mixing bowl, oiled

a baking sheet, greased

Makes 1 loaf and serves 6

Mix together the flour, yeast, salt and sugar. Gradually add in the water and 2 tablespoons of the oil, bringing the mixture together to form a sticky dough. Turn out onto a lightly floured surface and knead until smooth and elastic. Transfer to the prepared mixing bowl, cover with a clean damp kitchen cloth and set aside in a warm place to rise for 1 hour.

Break down the risen dough and shape into a large oval on the prepared baking sheet.

Using your fingers, press into the dough forming numerous small indents in it. Fill the indents with the tomatoes and olives and spoon over 2 tablespoons of the oil so that it fills any empty indents. Sprinkle with thyme and set aside to rest for 30 minutes.

Preheat the oven to 250°C (500°F) Gas 10.

Bake the focaccia in the preheated oven for 20 minutes, until golden-brown. Spoon over the remaining tablespoon of oil and sprinkle with salt.

Serve warm from the oven or at room temperature.

sauces, salsas and preserves

Classic tomato sauce

Very easy to make, this tomato sauce should be a staple recipe, handily made with store-cupboard ingredients. Serve it as it comes with pasta shapes or spaghetti and lashings of grated Parmesan cheese, or make heartier versions of it containing meatballs, chunks of Italian *salsicce* (sausages), fried aubergine/eggplant or slices of grilled chicken.

1 tablespoon olive oil

½ onion, peeled and finely chopped

1 celery stick, peeled and finely chopped

1 garlic clove, peeled and chopped

1 bay leaf

a dash of dry Sherry or dry white wine

400 g/14½ oz. canned plum tomatoes

salt and freshly ground black pepper

Makes 400 ml/ 1²/₃ cups

Heat the oil in a heavy-bottomed saucepan or pot set over a low heat. Add the onion, celery, garlic and bay leaf and fry, stirring often, for 5 minutes, until softened.

Pour in the Sherry and cook off the alcohol for 1 minute. Add in the canned tomatoes and season with salt and pepper. Increase the heat and bring the mixture to the boil. Reduce the heat and simmer uncovered for 25 minutes, stirring now and then.

Check the seasoning, discard the bay leaf and use as required.

Raw tomato sauce

A recipe this simple relies on good-quality ingredients, so choose the ripest, juiciest and most flavourful tomatoes you can find. Serve this fresh-tasting sauce with pasta spirals and grated Parmesan cheese for a wonderfully summery meal.

600 g/1¼ lbs. ripe tomatoes

1 garlic clove, peeled and left whole

2 tablespoons extra virgin olive oil

1 teaspoon balsamic vinegar

a handful of fresh basil leaves, shredded

salt and freshly ground black pepper

Serves 4

Begin by scalding the tomatoes. Pour boiling water over the ripe tomatoes in a heatproof bowl. Set aside for 1 minute, then drain and carefully peel off the skin using a sharp knife. Finely dice the flesh, reserving any juices, and transfer to a mixing bowl.

Add the garlic, oil, balsamic vinegar and basil leaves, and mix well. Season with salt and pepper.

Set aside to stand at room temperature to allow the flavours to meld. Remove and discard the garlic before serving.

Tomato passata

Homemade passata has a lovely fresh flavour and pleasingly silky texture. A versatile ingredient, use it in stews, soups, pasta sauces or, if reduced, as a topping for pizzas. Experiment with different herbs and spices to create your own variations.

1 tablespoon olive oil

1 onion, peeled and chopped

1 garlic clove, peeled and chopped

1 celery stalk, finely chopped

1 bay leaf

2 sprigs of fresh thyme

1 kg/2¼ lbs. tomatoes, chopped

½ teaspoon white sugar

salt and freshly ground black pepper

Makes about 600 ml/2½ cups

Heat the oil in a large, heavy-bottomed frying pan/skillet set over a low heat. Add the onion, garlic, celery, bay leaf and thyme and sweat for 3–4 minutes, stirring occasionally, until softened and fragrant.

Add the chopped tomatoes, mix in the sugar and season with salt and pepper. Increase the heat, cover and cook for 5 minutes, so that the juices come to the boil.

Uncover and stir well to break down the tomatoes. Reduce the heat and simmer uncovered for 30 minutes, stirring now and then.

Pass the tomato mixture through a fine mesh sieve/strainer set over a mixing bowl, pressing down well with a wooden spoon so as to extract all the tomato juice.

Allow to cool completely, then store in the fridge.

Sicilian tomato pesto

This Sicilian speciality uses local ingredients, including almonds, tomatoes and olive oil, to make an appealingly textured pesto, perfect for summer dining.

100 g/⅔ cup blanched almonds

250 g/½ lb. ripe tomatoes

1 garlic clove, peeled and crushed

a handful of fresh basil leaves, plus extra to garnish

100 ml/⅓ cup extra virgin olive oil

salt and freshly ground black pepper

freshly grated Parmesan, to serve

Serves 4

Toast the almonds in a small, dry heavy-bottomed frying pan/skillet until golden-brown. Swirl the pan regularly so that they don't burn. Remove from the pan and set aside. Once cool, grind finely.

In a food processor, blend together the tomatoes, ground almonds, garlic and basil leaves to a rough paste. Pour in the oil, season with salt and pepper and pulse gently to mix together.

To use, toss the pesto with freshly cooked, drained pasta, such as spaghetti or pasta spirals. Garnish with fresh basil and serve with grated Parmesan cheese on the side.

Tomato salsas

Nothing beats a simple, refreshing and appealingly textured relish, to serve alongside cold meat platters, atop hamburgers or as part of a Mexican feast. These four variations use the same tomato base to offer vibrant, colourful, tropical-tasting, summertime salsas that add a zing of flavour to any plate.

Tomato, apple and tarragon

300 g/10 oz. tomatoes

1 apple, peeled, cored and diced

freshly squeezed juice of ½ lemon

3 teaspoons finely chopped fresh tarragon leaves

salt and freshly ground black pepper

Tomato and sweetcorn

300 g/10 oz. tomatoes

the kernels from 1 cob/ear of corn

1 tablespoon finely chopped red onion

2 tablespoons chopped fresh coriander/cilantro

1 tablespoon olive oil

1 teaspoon white wine vinegar

a pinch of smoked paprika/pimentón

salt and freshly ground black pepper

Tomato and mango

300 g/10 oz. tomatoes

1 ripe mango, peeled, stoned/pitted and diced

4 tablespoons chopped fresh coriander/cilantro

grated zest and freshly squeezed juice of ½ lime

1 tablespoon olive oil

salt and freshly ground black pepper

Chilli tomato

300 g/10 oz. tomatoes

2 red chillies/chiles (see Note below)

1 garlic clove, peeled and crushed

2 tablespoons extra virgin olive oil

1 teaspoon balsamic vinegar

2 tablespoons chopped fresh coriander/cilantro

salt and freshly ground black pepper

All serve 4

For each of the salsas, halve the tomatoes and scoop out the soft seedy pulp, creating tomato shells. Finely dice the tomato shells, discarding the hard, white, stem base.

In a bowl, toss together the diced tomato and the remaining ingredients. Season with salt and pepper, and serve.

Note

To prepare the chillies/chiles, grill/broil them until charred on all sides. Wrap in a plastic bag (so that the steam will make them easier to peel) and set aside to cool. Once cool, peel, deseed and finely chop the chillies/chiles, being careful to wash your hands thoroughly after handling. Once prepared, use the chopped chillies/chiles following the method as above.

Preserving tomatoes

During the summer months, when tomatoes are traditionally abundant, the phrase 'tomato glut' is often applied to this prolific vegetable fruit. Not surprisingly, therefore, there are many traditional ways of capturing the tomato plant's natural bounty, transforming through preserving into tomato-based foods which can be safely stored and kept for many months. Over the centuries, long before the days of freezers and refrigerators, human beings have developed several ingenious ways of preserving the summer's harvest of vegetables and fruits. Nowadays, of course, freezing is one extremely simple way of storing tomatoes, with whole or peeled tomatoes, stored either in freezerproof bags or containers, kept in the freezer to be used for future cooking in sauces, soups or stews.

Tomato chutneys, in which tomatoes are cooked with vinegar, sugar, salt and spices in order to extend their keeping qualities, are a classic way of dealing with an excess of fresh tomatoes. Making your own tomato chutney at home is very simple, but there are a few points to bear in mind. When making a tomato chutney, because of the vinegar in the recipe, make sure to cook it in a non-reactive pan. Chutney making is not something to be rushed – take your time and cook it slowly in an open pan, stirring often, especially towards the end of the cooking time, so as to achieve a full, rounded flavour. Patience is also required before consuming it; store your chutney in a cool, dark, dry spot and allow it to mature. Given these simple pointers, though, tomato chutney-making allows for much happy experimentation, whether in the type of vinegar used, the other ingredients added (such as onions and apples) or the mixture of spices added for flavour.

Italy, with its warm, sunny climate, is a country in which tomatoes grow wonderfully well. Italian cuisine, deeply rooted in seasonality and the frugal, thrifty traditions of rural communities, has a number of ways of transforming and storing an abundance of tomatoes. Classically, fresh, ripe tomatoes are transformed into *salsa di pomodoro*, tomato sauce, or tomato passata/strained tomatoes, sieved tomato purée/paste, which is then bottled and sealed for use during the winter months. Drying tomatoes is another method the Italians use for preserving them. Traditionally, fresh tomatoes in southern Italy were dried simply and naturally in the hot sunshine, a process which enhances their flavour while creating a distinctive, chewy texture in the desiccated tomatoes.

Making either sun-dried or sun-blush tomatoes yourself is very easy, requiring just time, and the results are satisfyingly tasty. See methods opposite.

Sun-dried tomatoes

Traditionally, as their name makes clear, sun-dried tomatoes are made by drying tomatoes in sunshine. For those of us not blessed with a warm, dry and sunny climate, it is possible to dry tomatoes at home in the oven instead. Again, as with sun-blush tomatoes, the drying time varies according to the size of the tomatoes. The advantage of making your own dried tomatoes in this way is that they have a fresher, fruitier flavour and are far less salty than most commercially sold sun-dried tomatoes, with a rich sweetness and pleasant chewiness to them.

600 g/1¼ lbs. ripe but firm tomatoes, halved

salt

sugar

a baking sheet fitted with a wire rack, oiled

Makes about 500 g/18 oz.

Preheat the oven to 110°C (225°F) Gas ¼.

Using a small teaspoon scoop out the soft pulp and seeds of the tomatoes, forming tomato shells.

Sprinkle a tiny pinch of salt and sugar into the middle of each tomato shell. Place the tomato shells cut side-down on the prepared rack over the baking sheet.

Bake in the preheated oven for 6–10 hours, turning them over after 3 hours. The tomatoes will slowly dry out, taking on a wrinkly appearance. After 6 hours, check their progress every hour. What you are looking for is tomatoes which have dried out but without becoming overly brittle.

Allow the tomatoes to cool and store in an airtight container in the fridge, and use within a few days.

Sun-blush tomatoes

Sun-blush tomatoes are tomatoes which have been partly dried out, so they still retain some moisture. Cooking them in this way intensifies their natural flavour and sweetness, transforming even the dullest supermarket tomatoes into a treat. Bear in mind the simple rule of thumb that the larger the tomatoes are, the longer they will take to dry out. For example, cherry tomatoes, treated in the same way as ripe tomatoes here, are ready in about 2 hours. Use sun-blush tomatoes in pasta sauces, salads or as toppings for pizzas (see Triple tomato pizza on page 137).

450 g/1 lb. ripe but firm tomatoes, halved

1 teaspoon olive oil

a pinch of salt

a pinch of sugar

a pinch of dried oregano or basil

Makes about 300 g/10 oz.

Preheat the oven to 110°C (225°F) Gas ¼.

Place the tomatoes skin side-down on a baking sheet. Sprinkle evenly with the oil, salt, sugar and dried oregano or basil.

Bake in the preheated oven for around 3½ hours, until they have softened and partly dried out.

Allow the tomatoes to cool and store in an airtight container in the fridge, and use within a few days.

Spiced red tomato chutney

This nicely spicy, rich chutney with a touch of heat is great with hamburgers.

3 cardamom pods, lightly crushed

3 whole cloves

1 cinnamon stick

1 kg/2¼ lbs. ripe tomatoes, chopped, juices reserved

700 g/1½ lbs. cooking apples, cored and finely chopped

300 g/10 oz. onions, peeled and finely chopped

2 garlic cloves, peeled and chopped

a 2.5-cm/1-in. piece of fresh ginger, peeled and finely chopped

1 fresh red chilli/chile, finely chopped

200 g/1⅓ cups sultanas/golden raisins

200 g/1 cup soft brown sugar

300 ml/1¼ cups white wine vinegar

2 teaspoons salt

a sterilized glass jar

Makes about 1.7 kg/3 pints

Wrap the cardamom pods, cloves and cinnamon stick in a small piece of muslin/cheesecloth to form a spice bag. Put the spice bag and all the other remaining ingredients in a large, non-reactive pan set over a medium heat.

Cook, stirring, until the sugar has dissolved. Cover and bring to the boil, then uncover and simmer for 2–3 hours, stirring now and then, until the mixture has reduced and thickened, with little excess moisture. Test the consistency by passing a wooden spoon through the mixture; if it leaves a clean channel as it passes, the chutney is ready.

Remove the spice bag and bottle at once in warm, sterilized jars. Seal with new lids and clean screwbands. Keep in a cool, dry place for 4–10 weeks to mature before eating. Once opened, store in the fridge.

Green tomato chutney

Unripe 'green' tomatoes, with their firm texture and slightly sour flavour make an excellent tangy chutney.

1 cinnamon stick

4 whole cloves

4 allspice berries

5 [black] peppercorns

1 kg/2¼ lbs. green tomatoes, chopped

750 g/1¾ lbs. cooking apples, peeled, cored and finely chopped

300 g/10 oz. onions, peeled and chopped

150 g/1 cup sultanas/golden raisins

300 g/1½ cups light brown sugar

2 teaspoons salt

350 ml/1½ cups white wine vinegar

½ teaspoon Turkish/Aleppo pepper flakes

a sterilized glass jar

Makes about 1.4 kg/2½ pints

Place the cinnamon stick, cloves, allspice and peppercorns in a small muslin/cheesecloth bag. Put the spice bag and all the other remaining ingredients in a large, non-reactive pan set over a medium heat.

Bring the mixture to the boil and cook uncovered, stirring now and then, for around 3 hours until it has thickened and reduced, but still has a little excess moisture.

Bottle and store following the instructions to the left.

Tomato vanilla jam

Serve this jewel–red, sweet preserve, with its subtle vanilla flavour, as an appealing addition to the breakfast table. Enjoy it on bread, toast or pancakes, or stir into plain yogurt.

1 kg/2¼ lbs. ripe tomatoes

1 kg/5 cups jam/gelling sugar

freshly squeezed juice of 2 lemons

1 vanilla pod/bean

a preserving pan or large pan

sterilized glass jars

Makes about 1.3 kg/2¼ pints

Begin by scalding the tomatoes following the instructions on page 17. Roughly chop, reserving any juices.

Put the chopped tomatoes with their juices in a large mixing bowl with the jam/gelling sugar, lemon juice and vanilla pod/bean. Cover and set aside to macerate for 2 hours.

Meanwhile, place two small side plates in the fridge to use for the setting test.

Transfer the mixture to a preserving pan set over a low heat. Warm, stirring, until all the sugar has dissolved. Increase the heat and bring to a rolling boil. Cook the jam/jelly for 6–10 minutes. Test for setting point by turning the heat off and placing a teaspoon of the mixture on one of the fridge-cold plates. Leave for 30 seconds, then push the jam with a spoon. If the surface of the jam/jelly on the plate wrinkles, then jam is ready to bottle. If not ready, continue simmering the jam and test again in 5 minutes. Once setting point has been reached, remove the pan from the heat and set aside for 15 minutes.

Skim off any film, then bottle and store following the instructions on page 155.

Thai tomato jam

Thai lime leaves and lemon grass add a delicious fragrance to this spicy tomato jam; delicious served with hamburgers, grilled meat or poultry.

500 g/1 lb. tomatoes

1 fresh red chilli/chile, deseeded

1 garlic clove, peeled and chopped

a 5-cm/2-in. piece of fresh ginger, peeled and chopped

2 Thai lime leaves, central spines removed and shredded

1 tablespoon Thai fish sauce

100 g/½ cup caster/superfine sugar

50 g/¼ cup dark brown sugar

1 lemon grass stalk, pounded

Makes about 430 g/¾ pint

In a food processor, blend together the tomatoes, chilli/chile, garlic, ginger and lime leaves to a purée/paste.

Place the resulting purée/paste in a heavy-bottomed saucepan or pot set over a medium heat. Mix in the fish sauce, both sugars and the pounded lemon grass stalk.

Bring to the boil, stirring all the time. Reduce the heat and simmer uncovered for 1 hour, stirring often to ensure even cooking, until the mixture has thickened and reduced.

Remove and discard the lemon grass stalk and bottle at once in warm, sterilized jars. Seal with new lids and clean screwbands.

Keep in a cool, dry place. Once opened, store in the fridge.

Index

Credits

Page 21 ph: Erin Kunkel
Page 38 ph: Peter Cassidy
Page 72 left ph: Peter Cassidy
Page 72 right © AGF Srl / Alamy
Page 94 © Photocuisine / Alamy
Page 117 © Maximilian Weinzierl / Alamy
Page 152 ph: Jan Baldwin

Acknowledgments

My thanks for their kind help with the book to Mark Diacono, Nancy Gaudiello, Andreas Georghiou, Gary and Jenny Griffiths, Zoe Hewetson, Gary Ibsen, Rosemary Moon, Paola Nano, Newington Green Fruit & Vegetables, Esteban Andrès Soto and Ray Warner. It's been a pleasure to work on creating a book with the Ryland Peters and Small team. My thanks to Cindy Richards and Julia Charles for commissioning the book and Stephanie Milner for editing it. The book looks lovely – my thanks to Peter Cassidy for his mouthwatering photography, Lizzie Harris and Joanna Harris for styling, Sonya Nathoo for designing the book, Leslie Harrington for art directing, Sarah Kulasek-Boyd for her production work, and, in advance, to Lauren Wright for her hard work in publicising it.